The $447 Million Secrets of Sport

Discover the most powerful ancient and modern mind secrets used by the world's top sports stars.

P.S. These secrets can work in the rest of your life too!

Dedication:

This book is dedicated to my personal and online clients. Coaching is always a dynamic process, where the coach learns at least as much as the client. I have never tired of their questions, their aspirations, and the work we have done together in our efforts to move ourselves to at least the next level of achievement.

These clients have provided the challenges that fascinated and inspired me to explore the power and limits of the human mind. If we are able to use the word 'possible' in our conversations and thoughts more than the word 'impossible' we will have made a tremendous start in pushing back these barriers. We will also have a lot more fun in our lives.

This book is also dedicated to the featured athletes and their tremendous coaches. Their genius adds glorious colour and inspiration to all our lives.

Acknowledgements:

This book would not have been possible without the unwavering support and patience of my family as I pursued my passion to understand more about the human mind, and how we can all use it more effectively.

I am also extremely grateful to Martin Cooper, Ian Hagues, and Tony Wrighton for their generous editorial assistance. There were far too many typos, spelling mistakes, and grammatical errors in the draft manuscripts, and structural issues too. How do they find so many places to hide?

Martin, Ian, and Tony tenaciously hunted them down, and those that remain are entirely my responsibility.

About The Author

Dr. Stephen Simpson is a medical specialist, MBA, and Fellow of the Royal Society of Medicine. He works as an elite performance coach, and has written and presented many scientific papers at international conferences, as well as making frequent guest appearances on TV and radio.

His clients include leading names from the world of sport, business, and the entertainment industries.

Dr. Simpson is also a bestselling book and audiobook author and presenter. Full details can be found on his website www.drstephensimpson.com

Contents

Introduction

So you want to discover some secrets that you can use in your favourite sport to take your game to at least the next level? Excellent, you will find many in this book. It does not matter if your favourite sport is darts, badminton, or hockey, as these secrets can be adapted to any sport. Nor does it matter if you are not interested in the sports that I have chosen. It is the secrets that will be important for you.

Perhaps you are just interested to know more about the greatest superstars, and discover the magic ingredients that are the secret of their success? That is also excellent.

Would it surprise you to know that these secrets will work for you in the rest of your life too? At work, with your leisure activities, and with your personal relationships? It is true. These secrets will work in all of these areas, and you will have a lot more fun too. Sounds too good to be true? It probably does, but it is certainly possible. It will take some commitment from you, but probably less than you might imagine.

Avoid The Usual Mistakes

One of the biggest mistakes we make in life is clinging to our belief that we can only succeed the hard way. We have been brainwashed into thinking that success comes only from hard work, pain, will power, and many hours, months or even years of intensive training.

There is no doubt that dedication, persistence, and perseverance are required, but even so success can come a lot more easily than you imagine. The reason that you may not be fulfilling your expectations is because you are not using your most powerful weapon at even a fraction of its potential. This weapon is your imagination, and your unconscious mind skills.

So where do you start? Always look for the easy way. Avoid at all costs the temptation to reinvent the wheel. What does a child do when he or she wants to learn how to swim? He or she watches an older friend, and copies what they are doing. This will be much more fun than splashing around the pool for hours, coughing and choking, until the child learns how to swim by trial and error.

Another of our biggest mistakes is that we have not used the hard won lessons from the greatest thinkers and performers of the past. There is very little that is new in life, and yet each generation is convinced that it is smarter than the previous one. The result is that we still face the same problems, and it sometimes feels as if our life is going round in circles like a huge merry-go-round. So your life will be easier and richer when you study the best athletes in the world, and adopt some of their successful habits.

The Secrets

In this book you will discover the secrets of success that I believe are being used by our top athletes. The athletes themselves may be unaware of them, as these secrets are by definition unconscious. However, these secrets are the ones that I believe they use most effectively, and make them the best role models to study. The great thing about sport is that it is all about personal opinions, and so we are all experts. These are my choices, but I equally value yours too.

Choose the suggested secrets that most strongly resonate with you, and use them in your favourite sport. You will have more fun, and post better results. As an extra bonus you will delight in seeing with your own eyes that these secrets work just as well in the rest of your life too!

I have chosen the ten most popular international sports. I then identified the highest paid performer in the twelve months up to May 2012 in each one, using the illuminating Forbes World's Highest-paid Athletes list. The earnings totals are derived from salaries, bonuses, prize money, appearance fees, and licensing and endorsement income. I then dug deeper to discover at least some of the possible secrets of their success so that you can study them, and start to use them immediately.

It is also a matter of debate whether assessing an athlete's ability can be measured by how much they earn, but it is nevertheless a benchmark. Sport is increasingly big business, and money usually follows talent very accurately. We will all have our views about which sports to include, and who are the brightest stars, but this is my list.

I did bend the rules by including athletics sprinter Usain Bolt. He earned, by comparison with the others, a paltry $20 million. My justification for including Bolt is that he is such a powerful role model for our study, and in any case, will probably soon close the monetary gap with the others.

How To Use This Book

These are my recommendations of how to get the most out of this book, although I readily accept that everybody has their own preferred methods of study.

- Read only one chapter at a time, and then take a break of at least a day to reflect and internalise your thoughts.
- During your reading keep in mind the question of what could help you the most, and what resonates with you the strongest? Do not worry about how to use this information, as this fundamental question will be addressed later in each chapter.
- Write these best points down in the Scratch Box at the end of each chapter. There are several reasons why this is so important, and I will explain them later. For the moment I will just suggest to you that writing is the doing part of thinking.
- Ignore anything that does not resonate with you. There are so many secrets to choose from in this book that it is best not to waste your precious time on stuff that does not feel right. Trust your instincts.
- Keep an open mind about everything else. It might be helpful in the future, as we all assimilate new information and ideas at a rate that feels appropriate to us. Epiphany moments, sometimes called ‘Mind Pops’, can surface days, weeks, month, or even years later.

Each chapter comprises two main sections. The first section paints a high level summary of each athlete, their main achievements, and suggests some of their possible secrets. I have used information readily available in the public domain, and avoided negative opinion. This is a book about positive values. Nobody is a saint, and every human strength has a corresponding development area. You will think of other secrets that I may not have highlighted. Your own thoughts will be at least as valuable as mine, so jot them down too.

The second section of each chapter examines the athlete's suggested main secret in more detail. This includes simple explanations of how the mind works, and why some techniques will be much more valuable to you than others. You will discover how you can improve your skills in these vital areas, as well as exercises that you can deploy immediately.

Meet The Cast

So, here is the list of our top ten athletes, arranged in order of total earnings from salaries, bonuses, prize money, appearance fees, and licensing and endorsement income. The money adds up to a staggering $447 million, hence the title of this book.

The list lacks diversity with the notable and regrettable exception of any female athletes. Whilst they have won the battle for equal prize money, they have not yet attracted the lucrative endorsement and other revenue streams.

The marketing industry is surely missing out on a huge opportunity. The past lessons from the car industry, when it was assumed that only men buy cars, have apparently not yet been learned in the world of sport.

However, be assured that these performance secrets are equally applicable for female athletes, who can, and do use them, at least as effectively as their male counterparts.

1. Boxing - Floyd Mayweather - $85 million
2. Golf - Tiger Woods - $59 million

3. Basketball - LeBron James - $53 million
4. Tennis - Roger Federer - $53 million
5. Soccer - Cristiano Ronaldo - $43 million
6. American Football - Peyton Manning - $42 million
7. Baseball - Alex Rodriguez - $33 million
8. Formula One - Fernando Alonso - $32 million
9. Cricket - Mahendra Dhoni - $27 million
10. Athletics - Usain Bolt - $20 million

Scratch Box

Chapter 1 - Floyd Mayweather

Highlights

Floyd Joy Mayweather is an American professional boxer. He has won eight world titles, and unusually these were at five different divisions, or weights. This fact, and his undefeated record, underlines his claim to be amongst the best fighters of all time, and perhaps even the best. What is not in doubt is that he is certainly the richest, and indeed earned more during 2012 than any other athlete.

Boxing is both a brutal and yet artistic sport. Many of the best boxers are both highly intelligent and profound thinkers too. Entering the ring to face an opponent whose goal is to knock you senseless must concentrate the mind wonderfully.

A stereotype about boxers is that they took to their sport to escape the ghetto. With no skills or qualification there were few other options available to them. This stereotype is likely to be accurate in Mayweather's case. His background of severe social deprivation and fortuitously a family history rooted in boxing made his career an obvious choice. By coincidence he had unknowingly surrounded himself with the right people to ensure his success.

When the odds are so heavily stacked against success what are the special characteristics that fighters like Mayweather possess? When life is tough the options are limited, and so decisions are easy. As a German proverb stated,

'Whoever has choice has torment.'

Mayweather's goal from the age of nine was simple. It was to be the richest man in the world. It was a simple goal, and boxing was the only realistic way to achieve it. All of Mayweather's subsequent successes were a result of this one overarching goal.

Mayweather's nickname is 'Money,' and as is so often the case with nicknames it is uncannily perceptive. His boxing feats have stolen all the headlines, but it perhaps as a businessman that he should be most respected, and even feared.

Mayweather does not earn big money from the endorsements that athletes from the more glamorous sports enjoy. His money comes from fighting other boxers, and exceptionally in any sport, from promoting his own fights. He has tenaciously protected his rights, and this is the main reason why he is the richest athlete. His earnings from TV, film, and ticket sales are huge.

Equally important in a sport where the more you get hit the more long term damage you suffer, Mayweather does not expose himself to as many fights as his predecessors, nor does he need to. As he has pointed out on many occasions to his critics, the boxing world has changed. Its fans are prepared to embrace the exclusivity of their sport through the lucrative pay-per-view channels, and so there is much less pressure to stage numerous fights to generate earnings.

Mayweather has amassed a fortune, and arguably his biggest fights were outside the ring, protecting his rights from the promoters, agents, and managers. These are the people who may end up with much of a boxer's purse. They are extremely intelligent men and women, and for Mayweather to take them on at their own game and win is not much short of a modern day miracle.

So Mayweather has already achieved his childhood dream to be rich beyond measure. So what else gets him out of bed at night, as his habits are distinctly nocturnal? As so often happens with other athletes, his thoughts understandably have drifted towards the future, with the goal of leaving a legacy as a challenge for others to follow.

Such goals can be self-defeating, and generally whenever people move from the present, which they can control, to the future, which they cannot control, disaster beckons. As an example, golfer Tiger Woods has not won a

Major since announcing his dream of wanting to win more Majors than Jack Nicklaus.

So having a legacy as a goal can backfire. Mayweather wants to be compared with giants such as Muhammad Ali and Sugar Ray Robinson, and even to be considered better than them. This could be a much more effective goal, simply to be the best. 'I am the best' is one of his favourite expressions, and as a powerful affirmation works at many different levels of thought. It does wonders for self-belief too.

To be the best is about as simple as a goal can be, and is more powerful as a result. It can drive every thought, and provide motivation for yet another gruelling training session. There are many more attractive options, especially for one of the richest men on the planet.

'I don't care what fighter you're going to name, I'm the best,' Mayweather said. 'Throw a name at me and I'll break his stats down. Whatever they've done I've done it quicker, with no losses. The ultimate goal in boxing right now is to find a fighter that can beat Floyd Mayweather. And it's not going to happen.'[1]

Another goal that caused Mayweather much frustration and hence pressure, especially in his early years, was his quest for perfection. The pursuit of perfection has ruined many careers. Most successful people are perfectionist, and they move much easier to their flow state when they accept that they do not need to be perfect to win a fight or a boardroom tussle.

All that is required is to trust their thousands of hours of practice, coaching, and their innate ability. Athletes often talk about the importance of letting go, or getting out of their own way. It is as if they have another side of their personality, or alter ego, that performs much better when empowered to do so.

Mayweather has mastered this flow state. It is his autopilot during a fight that reacts faster than conscious thought, and so its source can only be unconscious or reflex. The hallmark of a great boxer is not how hard he can hit his opponent, although this helps. More important is how hard it is for his opponent to hit him. Mayweather and Ali at his peak were like dancers, light on their feet, hands held low, swaying from side to side like a snake about to strike, hypnotising and mesmerising their opponent, daring them to unleash their punch, knowing that this might be the last thing that they remember as their head hit the canvas.

Another benefit of locking into your autopilot is that it does not have emotions. Emotions are great for sharing with friends, but have no place in the ring. Mayweather is a superb controller of his emotions, and demolishes his unwary opponents with the clinical precision of a surgeon.

So Mayweather is a genius, as his achievements both inside and outside the boxing ring have proved. By any standards his early life would have broken most children's aspirations, but refined and tempered Floyd's.

The Big Secret

The secret that I have chosen for Mayweather is that he has such powerful goals, and as a result he has achieved the targets that he set for himself. They may not be perfect goals, but they do not need to be, and they have worked for him. The great thing about goals is that they can be changed, not too often, but when circumstances change.

The elegance of Mayweather's goals is that they are not only goals, they are also powerful affirmations. If you tell yourself the same thing enough times you will start to believe it, and then you are more likely to achieve it.

Mayweather's goals are simple. With his lack of options they had to be. They were to be the best, and to be rich, seriously rich. He has achieved both, and so is worthy of our study. Mayweather was also wise enough to recognise early in his career that chasing perfection as a goal would have crippled his development.

Goals will be a vital part of your success too. The first subject I discuss with clients is their goals. There is no other starting point. It is a happy coincidence that Mayweather is the richest athlete and so number one on our list. He is a perfect example to study when exploring the importance of goals.

However before you can set a goal, you have to know what you want, what you really, really want, as the Spice Girls sang. This requires accurate self-knowledge. Successful people know who they are, what they want, and how to achieve their goals.

Aristotle knew a thing or two about what makes us tick. He explained a long time ago,

'Knowing yourself is the beginning of all wisdom.'

Not surprisingly, successful people do know who they are, they do know what they want, and they do know how to achieve their goals. However the truth is that many other people struggle with developing and sustaining a sense of purpose, as did many of our ancestors too.

This is why this chapter is so important, and the logical starting point for your journey to sporting success. Not much has changed over the last three thousand years. When the same message of the importance of self-knowledge keeps surfacing repeatedly over the centuries, we can be fairly sure of its enduring value.

More recently Nietzsche described the difficulty attached to truly resonating with one's own unique personality. He would have known this more intimately than most people. Sadly he died in 1900 eleven years after suffering a serious nervous breakdown.

'One's own self is well hidden from one's own self; of all mines of treasure, one's own is the last to be dug up.'

The reason that self-knowledge is so important is that with it we can plan our lives, and develop authentic goals to structure order from chaos. Without self-knowledge we drift, or even worse, we waste our time and energy on goals that are meaningless, or beyond our control.

How To Choose A Wonderful Goal

Goals are therefore critical. If you do not know where you are going, then any road will take you there, and it may not be a happy journey. The skill lies in choosing the correct goal.

Ideally you should have one overarching goal in sport. I suggest that you take some time before deciding what this goal might be. It is very easy to think of an impressive goal, but is it the correct one? Is it something you want to achieve, or something that parents, teachers, or friends have recommended? Is it a goal that society regards as worthy, rather than something you have always wanted to do?

Motivational guru Tony Robbins gives a stark and somewhat nihilistic message of the dangers that haunt the unwary.

'You will become by and large what your friends expect you to become.'

This might feel like the easier path. To conform to others' expectations of you. However, we know on the inside when something is missing. In time this feeling builds dissatisfaction, and even stress. There is nothing more certain to cloud your judgement and performance than stress, especially if it is prolonged.

Mark Twain clearly observed similar lack of clarity amongst his circle of acquaintances.

'I can teach anybody how to get what they want out of life. The problem is that I can't find anybody who can tell me what they want.'

A good starting point is to ask yourself how you spend your discretionary time? What activity makes time fly, fills you with deep contentment either during or afterwards, and, in a humble and grounded way, you know that you are rather good at?

Bring Life To Your Goal

For most of your life at school, at work, and at home, you have been conditioned to a certain extent to recognise success by the monetary value of your possessions. Society sadly places less value on qualities that cannot be so easily measured, and yet are far more important.

There is nothing wrong with material goals. Most of us in the affluent world dream of big houses, big cars, and fat bank balances. It is all too easy to forget those who can dream only of the next meal.

So make your goal a means to an end, and the result of doing other things skilfully along the way. When you reach your goal, do not be surprised when you look back and realise that the real fun was the journey, and not the destination.

Tony Robbins makes another powerful point that deserves careful thought.

'Achieving goals by themselves will never make us happy in the long term; it's who you become, as you overcome the obstacles necessary to achieve your goals, that can give you the deepest and most long-lasting sense of fulfilment.'

Many mountaineers describe a sensation of anticlimax after climbing a particularly difficult mountain. They remember with much more lasting satisfaction the journey that took them there.

Certainly go for the dream of the big house, and enjoy it when you own it. However do not be surprised that once you own your new house, your goal has changed its shape, to a greater or lesser extent.

If it was for an even bigger house, then there may be many more house moves in store for you. If it is a new goal that germinated as if from nowhere, then perhaps you stumbled across an unexpected opportunity. This is what people call serendipity, coincidence, synchronicity, or just a healthy dose of luck. We will talk more about this in later chapters.

Back to the present. Once you have decided on your goal, the more different ways you can remind yourself of your goal each day, the more successful you are likely to be. There are many ways to do this. Examples include writing the goal on stickers and fixing them to the bathroom mirror, the refrigerator, using the goal as a screensaver on your computer, mobile phone, and alarm clock.

The more places you can think of to display your note, the more likely you are to reach your goal. It directs your unconscious mind, and helps to build a self-fulfilling prophecy. Keep in mind that writing is the doing part of thinking, and is a powerful connection to your unconscious mind.

'A goal properly set is halfway reached.' - Abraham Lincoln

Olympic swimming champion Michael Phelps is a great example of the importance of constant reminders. When he announced his goal of eight gold medals in the China Olympics he was incensed by reading an article expressing doubts that he could deliver his prediction. He pinned this article to his locker and stared at it every morning until he left for China. Was this visualisation? Was it a powerful affirmation? Was it a self-fulfilling prophecy? Who knows, but the important thing is that it worked for him.

'People say that I have great talent, but in my opinion excellence has nothing to do with talent. It is about what you choose to believe and how determined you are to get there. The mind is more powerful than anything else.' [2]

It certainly is, and each chapter will provide opportunities for you to explore your own mind in new ways. To open doors to your mind that you never knew existed. To open doors to more sporting success than you thought possible.

The Ultimate Goal Is Not To Have One

At the risk of further muddying these already murky waters, you might have guessed that the ultimate goal is to have no goal at all. When one's mind, body, and soul are seamlessly linked in the appreciation of the moment, then other goals are just not necessary. Magical results surface as if from nowhere.

Very, very, few people achieve this degree of detachment, and so the rest of us must continue to rely upon our goals. These are the goals that you have constructed with as much care and insight as you are able. They will be more than sufficient to provide inspiration during the journey.

We have enjoyed enough puzzles for the moment. Now review your notes and thoughts on this chapter. Ask yourself this question, 'What three things can I do now that can help me immediately, or at least in the very near future, to achieve the sporting success that I desire?

Our brains love questions, and the response is always more creative than when we just follow orders. Write them down now before you forget.

In the next chapter we will continue our journey, and examine the importance of finding the zone more often, and staying there longer. This is the home of peak performance, and vital to your sporting success. You will discover how the power of your thoughts can create a massive and positive effect on your performance. How meditation and hypnosis can promote the release of endorphins, and how they lead you to the zone. How sporting success is the result of getting out of your own way, and there is no better example than Tiger Woods.

Scratch Box

Chapter 2 - Tiger Woods

Highlights

Eldrick Woods is more commonly known as Tiger Woods, or just Tiger. He is an American professional golfer, whose fame spreads far beyond the narrow world of golf. Until recently he was the highest paid athlete in the world, although he has now slipped slightly to second place.

Golfers are judged by how many Majors they win, and there are four every year. Tiger collected his first Major in 1997 just a year after turning professional, and soon after was ranked as the best golfer in the world too. He retained this position for most of the next thirteen years. To date Woods has won fourteen Majors, and only Jack Nicklaus with eighteen Majors has won more.

Woods took time off from golf at the end of 2009 following his marriage problems. Not surprisingly his form slumped when he returned to golf in April 2010. Woods also lost some lucrative sponsorship deals during this time, denting his earnings.

Woods has many strengths, and one of them is his sheer physical presence. His competitors speak openly of being intimated when playing against him. Woods projects an aura of invincibility, and so often luck runs unerringly in his favour.

Another strength is his enormous physical power and his ability to hit the ball huge distances. This power comes from his intensive training, physical condition, and superb coordination. If players wanted to be able to compete with Woods one of the things they had to do was to match his training programmes. Golfers were until recently not noted for their physical training programmes.

Woods has mastered all areas of golf. These include long driving, accurate iron play, and recovery from difficult situations, such as heavy rough and treacherous bunkers. His putting is arguably his greatest playing strength, especially when under pressure. He appears to be nerveless, and has set records for the most number of consecutive rounds without the dreaded 3-putt.

Another example of Wood's mental strength is his ability to close out in the Majors. When he has been outright leader, or sharing the lead at the start of the final round, he has won fourteen times, and only lost once.

Wood's mother is a Buddhist, and so Woods was raised as a Buddhist too. He believes this has been the central foundation of his phenomenal development as a player and a person, not withstanding his recent difficulties both on and off the golf course.

Meditation is a central foundation of Buddhism, and so Woods would have learnt this skill from an early age. Meditation can be used in many different ways, but arguably its main benefit is that of facilitating control of the mind and the emotions. This is a priceless skill for any athlete to possess, and is the gateway to the zone. This is where mind, body, and soul combine as one, unleashing peak performance.

The Big Secret

The secret of Wood's success is that he appears to be able to enter the peak performance mindset known as the zone, almost at will. The key to enter the zone is meditation. The best example I have seen of an athlete describing the zone is from Woods. He uses phrases such as[3],

- Blackout moments
- Entrenched in the moment
- My subconscious takes over
- I don't remember the shot until the ball leaves
- It is a weird thing
- Things slow down
- The last few holes take forever
- I don't hear anything
- I am so involved in that particular moment
- I get out of the way
- I was sitting back and watching my body

If we did not know that Woods was talking about golf we would think he must be on drugs. He is – these are amongst the most powerful drugs known. They are not bought on the street, but manufactured within our brain. They include the endorphins, so named because their chemical structure is almost identical to morphine. However endorphins have none of morphine's dangerous side-effects, and are a powerful source of health, happiness, and control the gateway to peak performance. These are not new discoveries either.

'Sport is a preserver of health.' Hippocrates.

Endorphins were so named because their chemical structure closely resembles the synthetic drug morphine. The 'endo' part of their name simply means they are manufactured within the body.

Endorphins have been suggested as the chemicals released by long distance runners that gets them through 'The Wall', that produce pain relief during acupuncture, and that contribute to a sense of well-being during pregnancy.

Remember A Time When....

The effects of endorphins can be long-lasting, leaving an indelible imprint in our memory. When I work with athletes one of the exercises I use illustrates this point lucidly. I ask the athlete to close their eyes, and remember their best performance, in all its detail.

Their memory is almost instantaneous, even for events that might have occurred many years ago. Their memory is packed with information, often including the date and time of this event, and even the weather.

I then ask them to sum up in just one word what they felt during their event that was so different to their normal experience. Then the magic strikes. Their face and voice adopt a dreamlike quality, they smile, and struggle to find the word that describes what they felt then, often years ago, and what they are re-experiencing again now.

The result is not exactly earth-shattering, but no less powerful for its simplicity. Common examples are 'easy', 'calm', 'focus', 'concentration', 'quiet', and 'dream'.

When athletes describe the zone or peak performance other common factors emerge. They are similar to the factors that Tiger Woods described earlier in this chapter.

They include,

- Time distortion, either faster or slower
- Unaware of the external world, other people, and noise
- Little awareness of themselves, as if their body controls itself
- Detachment from the many worries and frustrations of ordinary life
- No judgement of self, others, or their performance
- 'Playing out of my mind'

During these moments almost all thought is unconscious, rather than conscious. This is why it feels easy. Anybody who has experienced the zone wants to experience it more often, and for it to last longer. To some it resembles in importance the search for the Holy Grail.

Golfer Justin Rose is another perfect example of this. He has learnt to meditate, and wrote after his maiden victory on the US Tour in June 2010,

'The crazy thing is that when you are in the bubble, you are not really conscious of what you are doing — so it feels relatively easy.

The key was to not chase it. I have finally got to the point where I am telling myself just to enjoy the game. Play it for what it is and don't fret about the results. In that way, I have discarded quite a bit of baggage.'

The control of the mind has been taken to the highest levels in martial arts, where body, mind, and soul combine to unleash peak performance. Competitors learn through meditation how to de-clutter their mind, and stay in the present, where both the past and the future are of little consequence.

So What Is Meditation?

The truth is that most of us will not spend months and years in deep meditation in search of sporting enlightenment, nor do we need to. We can learn some basic techniques far more quickly. Daydreaming is perhaps the simplest technique, and we all do it, when time allows. This downtime facilitates symbolic thought at a deeper level of the imagination, often approaching a spiritual playfulness.

Philosophers and scientists are classic examples of daydreamers. They pursue their dreams for the intrinsic pleasure this brings them, and they know the breakthroughs that often result. They may not call them sporting secrets, but that is surely what they could be.

Ignorance is not lacking the ability to see the world as it is, but rather ignoring what our senses and thoughts are telling us. Our minds are normally in a state of utter chaos. No wonder the quality of our decisions is often a lot less than we would wish for. We often hear ourselves, and others, complain that we are in two minds about the right thing to do. If only!

The reality is that we have millions of different thoughts competing for our attention at any one time. It is as if our head is crammed with an unruly parliament. Its members represent every possible shade of political opinion, and the member who shouts the loudest usually gets heard. This goes some way to explaining why we can reach two or more completely different decisions on the same subject within hours, or even seconds.

The ultimate goal of meditation is a quiet mind, where the parliament learns how to converse quietly, when the issue at hand is examined and debated from every conceivable viewpoint, when each member takes his or her turn to speak, when the others listen intently, when consensus slowly builds, and when the wisest member speaks last.

'Only in quiet waters do things mirror themselves undistorted. Only in a quiet mind is there adequate perception of the world.' Hans Margolius – German Philosopher

Intuitively, we would expect this mammoth process of meditation, daydreaming, and reasoning to take a huge amount of time. We would be wrong. This process can, in the right circumstances, take the smallest fraction of a second. It can even happen in a single moment, whatever that is.

Frustratingly, we never know whether this epiphany moment will take a second or a lot longer to surface until it happens. All at the rate and speed that is appropriate for the individual is a common explanation, and especially frustrating when we are in a hurry for sporting success. Unfortunately it can take far longer with an overloaded mind. In such circumstances decisions may take months, years, a lifetime, or even an eternity to germinate.

How Can You Use Meditation In Your Chosen Sport?

There are a wide variety of different meditation techniques. Many are often packaged as the only definitive method, and enshrine complex prescriptive instructions. It may take years to master these techniques.

However, this is a book about sport, where meditation is just one of the arrows in our quiver to perform at a higher level. So here are a few simple methods to experiment with.

In essence we are looking for a way to connect to our unconscious by quietening down our conscious chatter. Whilst ideally we would think of nothing, very few can achieve this goal, so a little direction can be helpful.

Before meditation give your unconscious a mission. Keep it simple, and an example might be,

'I am going to enjoy discovering how I can add 30 yards to my drive, slash two minutes of my personal best, or reduce my double faults by 20%.'

Some people find it helpful to stare at a candle as they drift away; others listen to their favourite chill music, or sit or lie comfortably with their eyes closed. Reciting mantras is another common technique.

A frequent question people ask me is if it matters if they fall asleep during meditation. I think not; the unconscious mind never truly sleeps. I have found that gently burning fires, especially camp fires, can also be deeply hypnotic. My eyes defocus without any conscious thought, and lead effortlessly to profound reflection.

I am as certain as I can be that others find the same benefits. All cultures appear to find sitting by fires in contemplation or quiet conversation pleasing. Whilst the security of light and warmth are obvious factors, the dancing flames and embers may work their magic too.

Developing a state of mindfulness is the overarching key to meditation. You do not need to practice all the methods listed above. Culture and personal choice dictate which technique is likely to be the most appropriate for the individual at any given time. Clearly one thing is for sure – it will be very difficult, if not impossible, to enter a state of meditation without adopting one of these techniques, or the many similar alternatives.

So how can you learn more? The good news is that you are spoilt for choice. Whole books have been written describing each of these examples of meditation. Reassuringly however these techniques are not as difficult to adopt as might be imagined. Courses are readily available in almost all parts of the world, and many of these are now internet based. It is likely to be the best investment in time you can make, and should not be too expensive either. If you are lucky it might even be free.

There are plenty of products to choose from. They include inexpensive music for relaxation and meditation, as well as self development and sports audiobooks. Guided meditations are especially useful, and I recommend them because they do not require any special training. You do not need to go on a course to experience the still mind that will result from these guided meditations.

The importance of breathing, and the different ways of breathing, have been known for thousands of years, especially in some cultures. HeartMath© is a powerful technique. It is a form of breathing control, and has many supporters. The techniques are simple to use, and are used by many athletes. Its use might explain how some athletes are able to slow down their heart rate when required. I practice these techniques every day, and have used them very successfully with clients too, and so they are definitely worth your consideration.

There is much valuable information available from the Institute, and even better, much of it is free. More details can be found at www.heartmath.org

So there is no shortage of options for you to explore.

In the next chapter we will continue our journey to the world of basketball, and discover how one player has learnt the importance of the control of his emotions to his performance.

Scratch Box

Chapter 3 - LeBron James

Highlights

LeBron James is an American professional basketball player. His many achievements include winning an NBA champion title. He was also the leading scorer for Cleveland Cavaliers, before he left in 2010 and joined Miami Heat.

This move at the time was controversial, but paid off for James, financially and professionally, when he led them to the 2012 NBA title. His playing form and leadership skills during this time convinced the experts that he was truly the current best player in the world. His name is mentioned in comparison with past stars such as Magic Johnson and Michael Jordan, and some feel that he is better than both, whilst others disagree.

His playing brilliance, warm personality, and stable personal and family life, have won him both respect and numerous lucrative endorsements. This has made him one of the highest paid athletes in the world.

To the surprise of those not familiar with the world of basketball he is also considered one of America's most disliked athletes[4]. This dislike is linked to the manner and timing of James's move from Cleveland to the Heat in 2010. Loyalty is prized more highly in basketball than many other sports, and Cleveland fans filmed themselves burning his shirt in disgust at his perceived disloyalty.

There are athletes who can turn public disapproval to their advantage, and enjoy playing the bad guy. However, these cases are the exception. James's demeanour changed, and the ready smile was replaced with an angry glower. His form suffered too, as could have been predicted. Authenticity is everything to peak performance.

In a Sports Illustrated interview in 2012 he explained how he was able to return to his winning ways. He told himself,

'This is what you love to do and you've been doing it at a high level for a long time, and you don't really need to change anything,'

'Just get back to what you do and how you play, smiling all the time and trying to dominate at the highest level. Do it with joy and do it with fun and remember that not too long ago this was a dream for you. Playing in the NBA was the dream. Don't forget that again. Just go out and improve.'

The Big Secret

James illustrates perfectly the connection between emotions and peak performance. If your emotions are negative or unstable you will find it very difficult if not impossible to find the zone. As a result your performance will be wooden, and lack the spontaneity, joy, and creativity of 'having your head in the right place.'

James was able to identify that his negative emotions were affecting his form, and indeed his whole life. He also knew that the surly persona he had adopted was far from his inherent happy nature. It is normal for people to turn inwards when they receive criticism from others, and the pain that James suffered from the hatred and bitterness that he received can only be imagined. For such a likeable person, supported by a loving family, the label of being America's most disliked athlete must have been especially painful.

Fortunately this period of black moods was relatively short. James was able to move on, exert control over his emotions, and his form returned. Unfortunately many people either cannot, or will not, make any attempt to control their emotions. As with all things of value it does take some commitment. However, if you use your head and follow some established methods it takes a lot less effort than you might expect.

So why are our emotions so important, and what can you do to keep your head in the right place?

The control of our emotions is so important because it has a direct effect each day on how much pleasure we experience, and the quality of our sporting performance. The two are inseparable. If we are in a bad mood our form suffers proportionately. Here is another example of the importance of emotions.

'A man who is master of himself can end a sorrow as easily as he can invent a pleasure. I don't want to be at the mercy of my emotions. I want to use them, to enjoy them, and to dominate them.' Oscar Wilde

A phrase I use with clients repeatedly is 'what goes on in your head comes out in your life.' Too often our thoughts become a self-fulfilling prophecy. If you want a different result then change your thoughts. Henry Ford's famous quote expresses this concisely.

'Whether you think you can or think you can't - you are right.'

Clearly it is going to make it much easier to reach your sporting potential if you think you can, rather than that you cannot. It is possible to direct your thoughts towards this positive mindset, but does require some practice. Author and social scientist Ralph Waldo Trine found that the best way to control his emotions was by adopting an active rather than passive outlook on his life.

'To get up each morning with the resolve to be happy... is to set our own conditions to the events of each day. To do this is to condition circumstances instead of being conditioned by them.'

Another way of strengthening this resolve is to construct your affirmations each day. What do you want to achieve, what are your goals? Make sure to aim high, remembering that what goes on in your head comes out in your life, and in the sporting arena. Usually your goal will be the maximum outcome that follows, and not necessarily the best that you are capable of.

'The enemy of the best is the good' is another of my frequent comments to clients. I use this phrase so often because people like their comfort zones, and are too easily satisfied by good results. They probably did not have to try a new approach to post a good time, or a good score. New approaches can be scary, because they are unpredictable, and so are the results, or lack of them.

However, sometimes the results arising from a new approach are surprisingly impressive, and much closer to the best that a person is capable of. This is why the enemy of the best is the good. This is why we need to be brave, and prepared to leave the safety of our comfort zone, even if only for a short time.

This does not sound too difficult, but to be able to have this resolve every day might be more problematic? This is the crux, and applies to all self development. It involves change. Anybody can change almost any behaviour for a single day, but to make a permanent change requires commitment and making choices. It is not as difficult as it might sound, and there are useful tools to help.

Before we examine some of the ways that will help you to exert greater control over your emotions, and cement in place a desired change, it will be helpful to know a little more about how your brain works.

The truth is that the brain remains one of the last barriers to scientists. Neurophysiologists have barely begun to unravel the secrets. What we do know is that we use but a fraction of our brain's potential. There are some parts of our brain that are rusty, or that we have forgotten how to use. As with any part of our body and mind we use it or lose it. This includes the control of our emotions.

So what are emotions? Emotions and gut-feelings are possibly shortcuts that the brain uses to process huge amounts of information and chunk them down to a more manageable size. The advantage is that this will speed up your thoughts and decisions. The disadvantage is that very often you will not understand why you acted in a certain way. You might even have experienced the same situation the previous day, and acted in a completely different way.

This can be very confusing. If self-development writer and lecturer Dale Carnegie is to be believed it is important to recognise that despite our love of logic, order, language, and rules we are fundamentally driven by primitive emotions, even though we may prefer to think otherwise.

'When dealing with people, remember you are not dealing with creatures of logic, but creatures of emotion.'

How you feel at any given moment depends on chemicals. Through the ages many have discovered the mind-altering properties of alcohol, cannabis, LSD, and legions of other external chemicals. Fewer have discovered the much more valuable and helpful secret that the body, especially the brain, manufactures its own chemicals that control your emotions.

These chemicals include neurotransmitters such as serotonin, dopamine, and noradrenaline. They are usually manufactured with perfect purity, and interact with each other in exquisite balance. This is just one of the many miracles in your body that is working in the background every moment of every day, and you are totally unaware of it.

The science behind these chemical interactions is staggeringly complex. Medicines have already been developed by brilliant scientists to treat conditions such as anxiety, depression, attention deficit disorders, Parkinson's disease, and schizophrenia. More medicines are discovered every year, and no doubt more Nobel prizes will be awarded in this area too.

These medicines can bring enormous benefit to patients, especially those with the more serious conditions. However the potential danger of any medicine is that it can reinforce the belief that there is a pill for every ill. This leads to a passive approach to our emotions and state of mind, with the risk that we forget that we can exert a degree of control ourselves over the neurotransmitters mentioned previously.

This will not happen overnight. For some reason a month seems to be about the minimum time required to cement a permanent change in behaviour, so that is the minimum time that you will need to commit to. By then any benefits should be clear, and you will not want to go back to your previous situation.

You only require a small shift in the balance between your conscious and unconscious emotional thoughts to stimulate production of more of the happy chemicals. Less conscious thought, more unconscious thought, a willingness to stay in the present, and the results will come. You will also be a lot happier, and happy people achieve much more than unhappy people, and this is especially true in sport. Roger Federer is another great example of a person who has developed supreme control of his emotions too, as you will shortly discover in the next chapter.

Scratch Box

Chapter 4 - Roger Federer

Highlights

Roger Federer is a Swiss tennis player, and is currently ranked the best player in the world, perhaps the best ever. He holds many records, but players are ultimately judged on how many Grand Slam titles they have won. Federer holds the current record with seventeen, and notably demonstrated his versatility and adaptability by winning on all surfaces. These are clay, grass, and hard courts.

Although Federer is now one of the top earning athletes this was not always so. He split with his management team IMG in 2003. This move was only partially successful, and he returned to IMG two years later. Unlike many athletes he adopts a hands-on approach to his sponsor contracts, and carefully selects them. He prefers a few long-term contracts to many smaller ones. Guarding his time is more important than the pursuit of money for its own sake.

Similarly he plans his playing schedule carefully, and plays less events than many of his peers. When he does play you can be certain that he is there to win. This unshakeable self-belief is his hallmark, and as a result he has won many matches from seemingly hopeless positions. Federer believes that victory in such circumstances is possible, and possible again is the power word.

In an interview with former player and current presenter Sue Barker he was asked how he reacted mentally when facing serve to avoid defeat. He replied that his priority was simple, to play the game the same as any other, and to avoid making any mistakes.

However, this strategy would not be enough on its own. He stressed that you also have to believe in miracles. Further, you have to make your miracle happen. He went further still, stating that it is not enough to hope for the best. You have to push luck on your side.

This is an extremely interesting comment, and one that other athletes have also expressed in their own different ways. The belief that luck is not random, that we do not live in a random universe, and that luck can be manipulated when the chips are down are relatively common themes.

Another interesting observation is that Federer is noted for his flamboyant and relaxed style. This has not always been the case though. Earlier in his career his mood was volatile, and his temper would sometimes surface. He knew this detracted from his performance, and he vowed to never say a harsh word again. This helped his concentration, but was not as successful an approach as he had hoped.

So Federer modified his behaviour on court. He would continue to enjoy his flamboyancy, and celebrate his wins emotionally. Tellingly the biggest change he made was concerning his defeats. He adopted a 'don't care' approach. He always gave his best, so why should he beat himself up when his opponent played better, or when his luck ran out?

Perhaps Federer also has an undefined magic ingredient that the best of the best possess. Something that makes a person truly special. We will try to identify what this might be, and how you might be able to share it, even if only a little bit. A little goes a long way.

The Big Secret

Federer possesses many secrets, but the one that makes Federer so special is his uncanny ability to extricate himself from seemingly the most hopeless situations. His comments that I highlighted earlier are telling. That you have to believe in miracles, and that you have to push luck on your side. His 'don't care' approach is also telling. I don't know whether Federer has any knowledge of universal laws or not, but he demonstrates the essence of their teaching succinctly.

Some people just seem to be lucky. You probably know people who usually win the lucky dip prize, and find lost money on the street. Such people are described as having the Midas touch, or as people who if they fell in the river would emerge with their pockets stuffed with salmon.

Such people can be irritating, as they explain how they always expected to win the lottery, or be left a fortune by a long-last aunt. Another irritant is how some people can take up a new sport, and immediately post surprisingly good results. There is even a phrase that describes this phenomenon. It is called 'beginner's luck.'

Rather than be irritated it is worth looking a little deeper, to see if there are any ways we could increase our luck too. Perhaps beginners enjoy their luck because they play with no fear, or no expectations? Perhaps they have not yet had enough people tell them how difficult their new sport is?

Without question we live in a complex universe, and are buffeted by random events. It sometimes feels as if we are bit players in a huge game of chance, with no control over the present or our future. This makes us feel very uneasy indeed. If we are not in control then many bad things can happen to us, right?

This is perfectly true, but as usual our thoughts drift unerringly to the worst case scenario. Many good things can also happen, and sometimes our best experiences arise from pure chance. How good would it make us feel if we could impose some order on these random events, or even use them to our own advantage?

Many people now talk about universal laws as the ultimate form of control, and especially the law of attraction. This law proposes that our conscious and unconscious thoughts can influence external events. The best-selling film The Secret describes the law of attraction in more detail. It was released in 2006, and became instantly popular. Rightly or wrongly the belief 'that thoughts become things' resonated deeply with millions around the world.

The Law Of Attraction

The law of attraction instructs us that positive people attract other positive people to them. This is not too surprising. We all know people we like to be with, either at work or in our personal life.

We also know many people who we do not choose to be around. Such people are the habitual moaners, and see the worst in any given situation. They are the energy vampires, and best avoided. They attract their own circle of like-minded negative thinkers. In extreme cases their energy can be destructive, focussing on negative emotions such as paranoia, jealousy, and anger.

The law of attraction not only postulates that positive people attract other positive people to them, but also that positive events attract further positive events. The law goes even further, and proposes that positive thoughts can lead directly to positive events, even at considerable distances. If even a fraction of this statement is to be believed then the implications are immense.

Its devotees use their own models to describe the law of attraction, but the consistent message is that energy follows our thoughts. In some way this energy expands to influence the event that was the focus of our original intention.

Many grounded and pragmatic people who have never even heard of the law of attraction, let alone put it into practice, nevertheless believe some strange force is out there, working in their favour. The words they use include luck, coincidence, synchronicity, serendipity, fate, and karma. They explain that a particular event was meant to be, or that things just fell into place.

French surgeon Alexis Carrel won the Nobel Prize for Medicine in 1912. His techniques for rejoining blood vessels are still used in transplant surgery to this day. Surgery is by necessity a practical specialty, but Carrel was a controversial free thinker too. He also believed that unseen forces can shape our destiny.

'Intuition comes very close to clairvoyance; it appears to be the extrasensory perception of reality.'

These ideas are not original, and similar theories were proposed by Napoleon Hill in his book Think and Grow Rich. This book was published in 1937, and is still a best-seller, with over sixty million copies sold, so at least it worked for Hill. Many of its readers were convinced it worked for them too.

So how can you start to use the law of attraction to find out whether it can help you too? It will work for you, at least in part. This is because much is just common sense, and does not require any belief or understanding of metaphysics.

The Secret instructs us that all you have to do is 'Ask, Believe, and Receive', and let the power of the universe take care of everything else. For some people this is enough information, and they are probably already following this or a similar mantra. Others will doubtless require much more convincing. What possible explanation can be given to them? If there is an answer it is likely to be hidden deep within the unconscious mind.

Scientists now broadly accept the huge influence and power of the unconscious mind, and yet their research has not even begun to uncover the tip of this iceberg, indeed not even the uppermost ice crystal. On the one hand this is frustrating, but on the other it means that your opinion is just about as valid as anybody else's. Perhaps the law of attraction is yet another example of the unseen power of the unconscious mind.

Asking is no more than the vivid visualisation of your list of skilfully constructed objectives. Others might name such a list as affirmations, or more simply as a wish list. To the unconscious mind the distinction between reality and perception is blurred, to say the least.

Critically the difference between successful people and the majority is that successful people have created an intricately detailed representation of what they want, using all their five senses. This visualisation is so convincing that part of their mind believes this success has been achieved already.

Other parts of their mind fuel this overarching goal. They construct repeated rehearsals of the milestone events that will ultimately lead to this success. Putting this strategy into practice enables successful people to examine a forthcoming job interview or sales pitch from every conceivable angle. They develop exhaustive 'What if..?' scenarios. As a result they are rarely taken by surprise, approach such important events with grounded confidence, and often walk away with a lot more than they bargained for.

You can do the same. The fastest path to success is to follow what works for others. Not only does this include embracing their strategies, but equally importantly it involves binning the self-limiting beliefs that you and others have skilfully installed into your mind over the years.

Believing is just that. Believing takes a leap of faith, and requires an open mind. Most of us have been persuaded over the years into believing that success comes only from hard graft, that practice makes perfect. If something sounds too good to be true, then it is too good to be true.

All of these statements are true most of the time, but they are not always true. How is it that some people float through life with a smile on their face, are very successful, and make it all look so easy?

It is because they have found ways to stack the odds in their favour. They are good at asking, and they are able to truly believe in their eventual success. This is the self-belief that is such an important ingredient of Federer's success. Indeed all top athletes share such unshakeable self-belief.

Receiving is also a tricky concept to explain. Sometimes it is easier to give a gift to another than to receive one yourself. The law of attraction requests that we watch for signs, that we interpret the events around us within the context of what we have asked for. That reception is an active process, and not a passive one. Receiving is not waiting for the universe to tap you on the shoulder with a wonderful gift. The gift is already out there waiting for you; you just have to find it.

One thing is for sure, we all miss a huge amount of vital information that is right in front of our faces. Information that could change our lives. More accurately we do not miss it – these signals are processed literally just behind our face, but often with critical errors.

Our mind takes multiple huge shortcuts, and largely 'sees' what it expects to see, based on previous experiences. This is why it is so difficult to see a hologram for the first time. The image is there, and processed accurately by the visual pathway. Yet it is rejected by the higher brain centres because it does not fit the expected pattern.

When we see, hear, or feel something that is beyond our normal experience it is rejected by our conscious mind. Yet the echo of this memory still persists in our unconscious mind. It causes a feeling of uneasiness, similar to the irritation of an unfinished conversation, until it finds the right environment to surface. This is one example of intuition, and like any other skill, can be improved with practice. Poet and author Robert Graves knew its value.

'Intuition is the supra-logic that cuts out all the routine processes of thought and leaps straight from the problem to the answer.'

The lesson here is clear. Open your mind to as many sensory signals as you can, and search for any clue relevant to your desire. The only way you can do this is by putting all your attention in the present, and this takes much practice. Resist the pressure to be dragged back into a blinkered view of the world that has been conditioned and reinforced by previous failed outcomes.

Be prepared to experiment with different options. It is not likely that success will arise from repeating previous unsuccessful efforts. Indeed Einstein defined insanity as doing the same thing repeatedly, and expecting different results.

Trust your intuition and instincts, but always ask yourself, 'What is the risk?' This is the safety net, because while instincts are often proven to be correct, there are occasions when they can be spectacularly misplaced, with potentially dire consequences.

Whether you can accept the possibility that the law of attraction can work for you, or maybe not, why not try it and see? Within the context of attempting to fulfil your sporting potential the truth is that living life with a positive attitude has got to be a lot more fun than expecting everything to go wrong. This is sometimes described as the 'half full bottle' mind set, as opposed to the 'half empty bottle.'

Luck is often mentioned in the same breath as the law of attraction. As mentioned previously, some people seem to be lucky at whatever they do. We can all think of examples of people who we know that sail through life getting all the lucky breaks. What is the source of their luck?

Howard Schultz, CEO of Starbuck's, believes we make our own luck by our own efforts, without the need for a mystical explanation.

'I believe life is a series of near misses. A lot of what we ascribe to luck is not luck at all. It's seizing the day and accepting responsibility for your future. It's seeing what other people don't see and pursuing that vision.' [5]

Self-development guru Paul McKenna also believes we create our own luck, and studies successful people to identify their secrets. He writes,

'Whether you choose to believe in the law of attraction or not, it's interesting to note that many highly successful people do.'

So at the very least these ideas merit further reflection, irrespective of their current lack of scientific basis. The law of attraction has contributed to the success of many of its supporters, and can do the same for you too.

Is there a contradiction here? Surely the law of attraction is about thinking of the future, and what we want? Yet we have already considered the critical importance of staying in the present. How can both arguments be valid?

A possible explanation is that the law of attraction considers the future to have already happened. You have made your wish, and there is little more that you can do to fulfil this wish apart from stay in the present, do the best job you can, and wait. What will be will be. This is a perfect introduction to the law of surrender.

Law Of Surrender – So What?

There is another widely quoted universal law, known as the law of surrender. This law is also known in some sports as 'Letting Go', as Tiger Woods has mentioned, and was highlighted in an earlier chapter.

Some words are more powerful at the unconscious level than the conscious level. This is when the words communicate emotion rather than simple description. Best-selling author John C. Parkin argues that saying aloud words such as 'so what,' or 'I don't care' is a spiritual act. That it is the perfect western expression of the eastern ideas of letting go, giving up and finding real freedom by realising that things don't matter so much (if at all).

Dan Millman describes his interpretation of the law of surrender in his book as,

'Surrender means accepting this moment, this body, and this life with open arms. Surrender involves getting out of our own way and living in accord with a higher will, expressed as the wisdom of the heart.'

In other words, acceptance is not an excuse for failure, but more of an opportunity to triumph over adversity. Success happens when we stop forcing the issue. When individuals work this out for themselves, they move to a much higher level of awareness. They describe the physical and mental relief of 'letting go.' Sometimes this awakening arises not from developing a calm mind, but from personal tragedy. There are many examples of athletes who unexpectedly achieved great things as a legacy to a loved one.

Federer knows he has given his best effort even in defeat, so does not risk denting his self-esteem, or wasting precious mental energy, by beating himself up. It is this acceptance that produces calm, and at the same time encourages peak performance. Just taking the tennis match one game at a time, where no single game has any more importance than any other.

This is one example of how games can be won when they are all but lost. When victory can be snatched from the jaws of defeat. This is a subject that our next star also knows much about, the soccer player Cristiano Ronaldo

Scratch Box

Chapter 5 - Cristiano Ronaldo

Highlights

Cristiano Ronaldo is a Portuguese football player, and currently plays for Real Madrid. He holds numerous records, and has won many prestigious titles. He is a prolific striker, and is the first European league player to score forty goals in a single season, not just once, but twice in consecutive seasons.

Ronaldo has been described as the complete footballer, equally proficient scoring with his head, either foot, or even his body. He is also equally comfortable with static ball situations, such as taking penalties, free kicks, and corners, as well as tackling and dribbling at high speed. He is also extremely fit, and carries 3% less body fat than a supermodel.

Not surprisingly Ronaldo is one of the most popular soccer players in the world, and even less surprisingly, the highest paid. So what is the secret of his success? What goes on in his head, and how can you use this knowledge in your favourite sport?

The Arsenal manager, Arsene Wenger, offers some revealing clues. He describes the importance of Ronaldo's air of arrogance, and his belief that he is number one. This belief comes from the fact that he knows that he can do whatever it takes to succeed.

Where do you wish to draw your personal line between being arrogant, and possessing self belief? If you choose to err on the side of being too arrogant, rather than less be prepared to accept that it will lose you at least a few friends, (who never really were your friends anyway). It will also invite hostile media criticism. It is all a matter of balance, and personal choice.

Other revealing clues to the source of Ronaldo's success are highlighted in the documentary Ronaldo - Tested To The Limit. During this series of experiments scientists examined both his physical and mental performance, and he scored exceptionally highly in both areas.

One of the experiments involved wiring him to a special piece of equipment that monitored his eye movements whilst dribbling the ball past an opponent. It was expected that 80-90% of the information he processed from the environment would be visual in nature.

This experiment confirmed that Ronaldo's eye movements were extremely rapid, as he quickly scanned the ball, the defender's body parts, and areas of open space. The result was that he could predict the defender's movements, and intuitively read the game almost instantly, and certainly much faster than is possible using his conscious mind. These thoughts were coming from his unconscious mind, and Ronaldo trusts them implicitly.

This is another mind secret nugget, and one that most players get wrong as they attempt to use their conscious mind to make results happen. The truth is that the greatest gift is to trust and let things happen rather than make them happen. This mind strategy is sometimes referred to as 'letting go,' as mentioned in the last chapter, and releases the far greater and much faster power of the unconscious mind.

Another fascinating experiment involved taking a corner for Ronaldo to score from, using his head or foot, depending on the height of the ball. There was no goalkeeper or other defenders to obstruct his efforts, so this task should not have been too difficult, except that as the ball was flying about half way to him, the lights in the stadium were switched off. As you might have guessed Ronaldo was able to score comfortably, because his unconscious mind had accurately predicted the flight of the ball, and he was able to complete his final movements in complete darkness.

The scientists were determined to test Ronaldo to the limit. In the next experiment the lights were switched off just before the ball was kicked in his direction. It made no difference. Still the ball ended up at the back of the net, as

Ronaldo imagined the flight of the ball, using only the player's movements before the ball had even been kicked. Ronaldo was able to process this information by tapping into his unconscious memory banks. He could access all this information from thousands of hours of practice to recall the pictures he would need, in absence of a real ball that he could see.

This process is called visualisation. We are all capable of visualisation, but Ronaldo has taken it to its extreme level. As we study other athletes in this book the importance of visualisation will be demonstrated in many different ways. The good news for you is that it is possible to improve your visualisation skills, as you will soon discover. A little extra will make a huge difference to your success, and not just in sport.

If you wish to succeed, and perform at your highest potential always keep in mind that the enemy of the best is the good. Ronaldo has more money than he will ever need, but his drive for perfection lies much deeper.

'The base of my success is to improve all the time.'

The Big Secret

It was a tough decision to choose Ronaldo's most powerful secret. It could easily be his confidence, but on balance it is his visualisation skills that are the most extraordinary.

The importance of visualisation is talked about a lot in sport, and rightfully so. Less often do coaches explain to their clients how to visualise effectively. Rarely do constructed visualisations include details of touch, hearing, smell and taste. It is like the difference between looking at an old black and white photograph, and being the star in the middle of a Hollywood blockbuster movie.

Part of the reason most people's visualisations are so limited is the word itself. Visualisation infers that its use is restricted to what you can see. If the word is replaced with imagination, or even rehearsal, then all the senses are included. Not only are they included, but they can also be amplified.

Critically the difference between successful people, and the majority, is that successful people have created an intricately detailed representation of what they want, using all their five senses. To the unconscious mind the distinction between reality and perception is blurred, as has been previously noted. A powerful visualisation should be so convincing that part of your mind believes that this success has been achieved already.

The fastest path to success is to follow what works for others. Not only does this include embracing their strategies, but equally importantly it involves binning the self-limiting beliefs that we and others have skilfully installed into our minds over the years.

I will present some powerful examples of visualisation, and these will probably stimulate some thoughts about how you could use these yourself. I will then describe two exercises that you can use to further develop your visualisation skills and imagination. Finally I will reveal the secrets of how you can turbocharge your efforts to an ever higher level.

So here are some superb examples of visualisation. The first is from the greatest golfer of all time. He truly understood the power of visualisation – Jack Nicklaus. He worked this out for himself long before the armies of psychologists arrived on the golf scene. Let me give you one of his examples from his book Golf My Way.

'I never hit a shot, not even in practice, without having a very sharp, in-focus picture of it in my head. It's like a colour movie. First I 'see' where I want it to finish, nice and white and sitting up high on the bright green grass.

Then the scene quickly changes and I 'see' the ball going there: its path, trajectory, and shape, even its behaviour on landing. Then there is this sort of fadeout, and the next scene shows me making the kind of swing that will turn the previous images to reality.'

We can learn even more from Nicklaus. When he retired to his room in the evening, he referred to it as going to the movies. He would lie on his bed and replay his round, examining each shot, making edits, and finally watching his perfect movie.

As a result he would have real difficulty remembering the bad shots, because in his mind they had not happened, nor had they left a negative imprint behind. Not surprisingly, he would construct a perfect movie of the next day too.

Dr. Simon Jenkins (Principal Lecturer in Sports Coaching) describes mental practice as,

'Covert (rather than overt) practice of a skill in that no actual movement occurs. It involves the use of imagery and verbal thoughts.'

Skiers do the same too. Physiologists have wired their muscles, and attached them to recording machines. This is called electromyography. They discovered that when a skier is standing in the laboratory with their eyes closed, and visualising their next competition run, the same muscle groups are being flexed, and at the same time, as would happen on the real run, and accurately mirroring the ski terrain.

Jenkins confirms the value of mental practice too from a scientific standpoint.

'There is evidence to suggest that mental practice is better than no practice, and that mental practice in combination with physical practice is even better.'

This is good news for those who spend long days away from home, or who live in inhospitable climates. Play your favourite sport in your mind. If you are not yet convinced then this famous example may be the final convincer. It was written by Hirini Reedy, and is also quoted by Csikszentmihalyi, in his inspirational book, Flow.

'Major James Nesbeth spent seven years as a prisoner of war in North Vietnam. During those seven years, he was imprisoned in a cage that was approximately four and one-half feet high and five long. During almost the entire time he was imprisoned he saw no one, talked to no one and experienced no physical activity. In order to keep his sanity and his mind active, he used the art of visualisation.

Every day in his mind, he would play a game of golf. A full 18-hole game at his favourite course. In his mind, he would create the trees, the smell of the freshly trimmed grass, the wind, the songs of the birds. He created different weather conditions - windy spring days, overcast winter days and sunny summer mornings. He felt the grip of the club in his hands as he played his shots in his mind. The set-up, the down-swing and the follow-through on each shot. Watched the ball arc down the fairway and land at the exact spot he had selected. All in his mind.

He did this seven days a week. Four hours a day. Eighteen holes. Seven years. When Major Nesbeth was finally released, he found that he had cut 20 strokes off his golfing average without having touched a golf club in seven years.'

The final example of visualisation in sports is from another sporting superstar, this time from the world of boxing.

Muhammad Ali was perhaps the greatest boxer of all time, and developed powerful visualisation skills. One of my colleagues met him, and asked for the secret of his success. He sighed wearily, and explained again for the thousandth time,

'I float like a butterfly and sting like a bee.'

My friend understood the 'sting' but was still confused by the 'butterfly' metaphor. Muhammad Ali leant closer and whispered,

‘I imagine floating out of my body like a butterfly.’

He imagined that he was standing at each corner of the ring and watching the fight from above. When he saw a muscle ripple in the shoulder of his opponent he knew what type of punch was coming his way, and had more time to take avoiding action.

All successful people, not just those in sport, have superb visualisation skills. So do not hesitate to use these skills in the rest of your life too. Albert Einstein explained that most of his creative thoughts were in pictures, and that he rarely thought in words at all. This is surely proof that a picture, or visualisation, is worth more than a thousand words.

So now it your time to experiment with these ideas. Find a video on YouTube or elsewhere of one of the top stars in your sport performing one of the skills that you need to improve, or master to an even higher level. Even better is to make it loop so that you can watch it many times over.

When you feel ready close your eyes, and imagine stepping into the picture, and then float out of your body as Ali did, and into the body of the star. Imagine what it feels like to be that person. Enjoy performing their routines too. The more powerful your imagination, the more revealing and interesting your insights will be.

Make Sense Of Your Five Senses – Go Large With Your Movie

The next exercise puts you in charge of a major movie, and it is all about you. Great movie directors know the importance of creating vivid imagery using all of our senses. They are so important because they are your only information inputs from your environment – an environment that is limitless in its abundant diversity. These senses are all you have to make sense of your surroundings, and everything is channelled through these conduits.

We have five senses; what we see, hear, feel, taste, and smell. Now it is time for you to direct your own movie. Make sure it is packed with detail relating to your five senses.

So let us get the cameras rolling. Lie back, close your eyes, and imagine some competition, match, or event in the future, perhaps a few months away, something that you would really like to win.

Picture yourself receiving the trophy or the prize, and being asked to deliver the customary modest but eloquent winner's speech. Then reflect on all the things that went right over the preceding months to position you for your success in the competition. You recognise that your processes were sound, and that your journey was a series of small steps, and not all of them were in the correct direction, or so it seemed at the time.

Your thoughts are interrupted as a journalist from the local paper approaches you and asks you for the secret of the amazing improvement in your game. Could you pass on some tips that would interest and help her readers?

Pause for thought for a few seconds. Then share with her some of the most illuminating insights and suggestions that you found the most useful in winning this competition. Most people like being asked to help others, and this is another of the reasons why this simple visualisation can be so powerful.

What you have also done is change your perspective. You have permitted your unconscious mind to create a vivid movie of a positive outcome in the future. Furthermore you have also changed your perspective by being the observer, and watching yourself behave with unconscious excellence in this movie.

Whenever you consciously change your perspective you will always profit from this new viewpoint. Apart from anything else you will see yourself with greater clarity, and more accurately as others see you. The alternative is to continue living in a self-deluded world. It may appear to be a more comfortable world, but in reality it will always be a more restricted world.

Sometimes there is a danger that future goals can feel very remote, and may even discourage you from starting your journey. However, when projects are broken down into small steps suddenly the most impossible task seems much more reachable. Focus on process, and the results will take care of themselves.

Using Visualisation To Develop Self-fulfilling Prophecies

This is another exercise, and one of the easiest, because you do it whilst asleep. Life is a journey of discovery, and learning more about yourself, about your sport, and indeed about the rest of your life is not as difficult as it might sound. There is a time when the conscious mind is switched off for several hours, and this is when you sleep and dream.

For it is during this time that the deeper structures of your brain are working the hardest. It is when the events of the previous day are analysed and catalogued, and it is when remaining problems are examined from every angle, and it is often when breakthroughs occur.

I know many people who keep a pencil and a piece of paper by the side of the bed, and when they wake up at three in the morning with the answer to a problem that has puzzled them for a long time they write it down lest they forget it.

I'm not suggesting that you should do this, but I do suggest you give your unconscious mind a mission to tackle while you sleep and dream. A little direction is a good thing because otherwise the brain will start thinking its own thoughts, and these might not be so helpful.

Many people enjoy completing crossword puzzles, and believe that these puzzles keep their brains tuned, and even prevent ageing. One of my clients, Martin, often wakes up in the morning with the answers to difficult clues that had evaded him the previous night. He is convinced that his unconscious mind had found these answers as he slept. Many other people would agree with him. If our sleeping brains can find answers to crossword puzzles, then what else are they capable of?

Your brain is an incredibly powerful computer. Some people claim that every experience is remembered and never forgotten. Whether that is true, or not, it is certainly true that our brains remember millions of events that have occurred over the years.

For example, your brain can remember almost all the games or events that you have ever played. It can differentiate between the good ones and the not so good ones, and it can work out where the good results came from. So think of your bad experiences in a different way – think of them as great learning opportunities.

Suppose that you are faced with an important decision or problem – it could be about golf, or something completely different. Just before you drift off to sleep say to yourself, ‘As I sleep and as I dream I will examine this situation from every possible perspective, and enjoy finding the best answer for the authentic me.’

When you wake up do not be surprised if the problem feels less important or urgent. You may not have found a solution, but you will feel as if you have made a great start.

Master Your Moment

Now I will explain how to turbocharge the visualisation exercises that you have developed already. The greatest film directors understand the connection between your senses and your resultant emotions on an intimate and almost certainly intuitive level. The result of their control of your senses and emotions is that they also control your brain chemicals. A great film can take you through a complete range of different emotions, as can a skilfully choreographed sporting event.

You might be able to predict where this somewhat lengthy discourse is leading. This is it. You have all the skills you require to be the Master or Director of your emotions, and happiness. All that is required is to add some flesh to the bones of your five senses as you pursue your favourite sport.

Experiment with adding some of these embellishments to your sensory experiences. They are only suggestions. There are many others you can choose, or even better invent your own. They will be more powerful if they are your choices.

What You See
- Big
- Bold
- Bright
- Colourful
- Focussed
- Moving

What You Hear
- Music
- Sounds of nature
- Voices
- Other people

What You Feel
- Where
- What
- How much
- Constant or rhythmical

What You Smell And Taste
- Where
- What
- How much
- Constant or rhythmical
- Associated with other memories

Now go back to the previous visualisation exercises, and start filling in some of these details. This will give you a huge advantage, because many people struggle with visualisation. It is not that they cannot visualise, it is because they do not feel confident or competent. It is because they have not been taught how the top athletes have developed their visualisation skills, either through their own efforts, or by working with their coaches. Now you have all you need. Just do it. As usual the more you practice the better your results will be, as American football player Peyton Manning has discovered many times over.

Scratch Box

Chapter 6 - Peyton Manning

Highlights

Peyton Williams Manning is a professional American football player. He plays in the pivotal quarterback position, currently for the Denver Broncos.

Manning started his career with the Indianapolis Colts in 1998 until 2010. During this time the Colts achieved many successes, and these culminated in winning the Superbowl. Manning comes from a family with close ties to the game. His father was an NFL quarterback, and his brother Eli is quarterback for the New York Giants. Manning is widely regarded as the best player of the 2000 decade.

Athletes fear two things above all others, loss of form, and injury. Often they are directly linked. American football is an aggressive physical contact sport and serious injuries are common. Manning was an exception, and he did not miss a single NFL game until 2011. This was a run of 208 consecutive games. However, during this time he had been playing through an increasingly troublesome neck problem. It had caused him pain and arm weakness for several years.

In May 2011 the decision was made by the medical team that surgery would be required. The operation initially appeared to be successful, and in July 2011 Manning was offered a new five year contract with the Colts, worth $90 million. However his subsequent recovery was not as hoped, and further more radical surgery took place in September 2011. This involved fusing bones in the cervical spine. As a result Manning did not play a single game in the 2011 season, and was released by the Colts. His surgeons were far from certain when, if ever, Manning would play again.

However, Manning clearly expected to return to NFL, and signed with the Denver Broncos in March 2012 for a new five year contract, worth $96 million. He played his first game for the Broncos in August 2012, and scored two touchdowns in the opening match of the season, to take his total to 400. Dan Marino and Brett Favre are the only other players to have passed this mark, and Manning was the quickest of this trio to achieve this record.

So what are the secrets of success that have fuelled Manning's astonishing career? One of them is the courage with which Manning dealt with his career-threatening injury. Although it is not yet clear whether he will return to his best form, the early reports are encouraging.

It is a major achievement to be able to play football at all, and only Manning knows how many hours of training and rehabilitation were required. As well as courage, other qualities were also required. These included persistence, perseverance, and unshakeable belief that the best outcome was possible. That triumph can, and will, arise from adversity.

Manning's courage was also demonstrated by his earlier unbroken run of games, despite carrying an injury. Many other athletes would have rested, or played with the expectation that because they were injured, they would not be able to play to anywhere near their best. It takes a very special mindset to block out such thoughts, and is a gift that few have.

This does not mean to say that athletes should play through injuries. These are finely balanced decisions that require evaluation by both the medical support team and the athlete. However, the fact is that Manning did play and train through such an injury for several years, and without any noticeable loss of form. This fact is nothing short of incredible, and is the mark of a true champion.

The other quality that other players and coaches have recognised is Manning's anticipation. Manning could probably not explain how he knows what another player will do before the player himself knows. It is a combination of wide peripheral vision, acute observation of body language, confidence, visualisation, and an instinctive belief that these feelings can be trusted. This could also be a description of the zone, the mental flow state that is the natural home of peak performance.

It could also be described as an advanced visualisation, a gift that he shares with Ronaldo. Whilst this is undoubtedly one of his secrets, it would not have been of much use without another one. This is Manning's incredible ability to cope with injuries and adversity that would have ended most other athletes' careers much earlier.

The Big Secret

How strange! What on earth does adversity and illness have to do with reaching your sporting potential? Well, quite a lot. These are not topics we normally like to think about too much, but unfortunately adversity and illness will strike at all of us at some point during our sports career. How we deal with them will determine to a large extent our level of success, or the lack of it. Winston Churchill was in no doubt.

'We shall draw from the heart of suffering itself the means of inspiration and survival.'

As always it is well worth studying other people to find answers for ourselves. Specifically those who were able to triumph over adversity. It is a rare gift to be able to turn a negative situation into a positive one, which is why society quite rightly admires survivors. These are the people who beat the odds. We like to see the living proof that sometimes the odds can be beaten, and if they can do it, then perhaps so may we.

Manning's future in football had been written off by many experts, and they may yet be proven correct. Not only did Manning have to deal with the rehabilitation from the fusion of his neck bones, but also the problems of pain and weakness resulting from the damaged nerves that control the arm muscles. Nerves heal even more slowly than bone.

While Manning expected to recover in six months, the medical specialists knew that it would more likely be a year, or even longer. So it proved, and the intensive physical training and practice, much of it in private and on his own, were a testament to Manning's courage, commitment, and persistence.

It Is Good To Be Nice – But Not Too Nice

Dr. Lydia Temoshok is Professor of Virology at the University of Maryland Cancer Centre. Her career has focussed on the relationship between the mind and physical illness. Dr. Temoshok's research work with Dr. George Solomon in 1987 approached the interaction between mind and body from a positive perspective. They focussed on the HIV/AIDS patients who were long term survivors. They were able to identify eight characteristics that correlated with survival. These are:

- They are realistic and accept their diagnosis and do not take it as a death sentence.
- They have a fighting spirit and refuse to be helpless/hopeless.
- They have changed lifestyles.
- They are assertive and able to get out of stressful and unproductive situations.
- They are tuned into their own psychological and physical needs, and they take care of them.
- They are able to talk openly about their illness.
- They have a sense of personal responsibility for their health, and look at the treating health care provider as a collaborator.
- They are altruistically involved with other persons with HIV.

On this last point Manning has been a generous benefactor to disadvantaged children's charities throughout his career. This was not directly linked to his own injury, but it is quite likely that by working with sick children it put his own problems into perspective.

This research also stresses the importance of being assertive too, and taking control of our life where possible. The same findings have been echoed in many other studies. While such research continues to be controversial, few would argue that adopting the above eight steps can only help an individual come to terms with their illness. Anything else is a bonus.

So like it or not, we will all face adversity and illness at some point that will have an impact on our sporting performance. One of the irritating clichés people use is,

'Don't worry – good will come from adversity.'

They mean well, but these do not feel like helpful comments at the time. However, looking back they are often right. Very few great successes in life happen easily. More commonly they are preceded by months or years of increasing frustration. The other cliché that is often heard is,

'It was hard to believe at the time, but it was probably the best thing that ever happened to me!'

A similar comment was made centuries ago by one of the leading Roman poets at the time of Augustus, Quintus Horatius Flaccus.

'Adversity has the effect of eliciting talents which, in prosperous circumstances, would have lain dormant.'

I hope that you are healthy right now. I normally encourage only positive thoughts, but there is always an exception for every rule. This is it.

Spend just a few moments imagining how you would feel if you had just been told that the injury you picked up in training is more serious than first thought. The medical specialist insists that it will take a minimum of one year to heal, if ever. You may never be able to play your favourite sport again, or at the same level. How would you use this time? What would you do differently? What would each day look and feel like?

Now reorientate yourself back to your present situation. Are any of the changes you considered just a few moments ago still appropriate? If so, what would it take to make them possible?

In an interview with The New York Times in September 2012 Manning was asked about his future.

'I'd like to be the player that everybody thinks they are used to seeing,' he said. 'I want to be the player that they're used to seeing. Is that possible? I'm going to work hard to be best player I can be. You've got to fight carrying that burden.'

Apart from demonstrating persistence this is another example of the use of the power word 'possible.' If you accept advice from others that the situation is impossible then that is what will happen. Manning never has accepted impossibility, and whilst he continues to use the word 'possible' all options remain open, and provide fire for his continued intensive rehabilitation.

Baseball player Alex Rodriguez has also had to rehabilitate himself, but in rather a different way, as we will discover in the next chapter.

Scratch Box

Chapter 7 - Alex Rodriguez

Highlights

Alexander 'A-Rod' Rodriguez is an American professional baseball player. He is considered to be one of the best players of all time. He has established many records, not least being the youngest player to hit both 500 and 600 home runs in his career.

Rodriguez also set the record for being awarded the richest contract. In 2007 the New York Yankees agreed a 10 year contract for his services worth $275 million.

His exploits on and off the field have attracted huge publicity, and sometimes controversy. In 2009 he admitted to using steroids from 2001 - 2003 when playing for the Texas Rangers. Rodriguez was named when the results of an anonymous drug testing programme were made public. To his credit he did not complain about this serious breach of confidentiality, and accepted sole responsibility for his actions. He now performs charitable work educating children about the dangers of drug abuse.

Rodriguez's personal life has also been volatile, and these incidents do not appear to have affected his playing performances.

Confidence is an absolute requirement for peak performance, and can be an elusive resource. Willpower alone cannot create it, and its authenticity comes only from extensive preparation. Ten thousand hours is widely quoted as the minimum time required to be proficient at any task. This figure should not be taken as an absolute because there are fast ways to learn as well as slow ways, so it may be more, or it may be less. Either way Rodriguez knows the importance of preparation.

'This is how I define grace: you're on the main stage, and it looks like it has been rehearsed 100 times, everything goes so smoothly. That's where I get my confidence and success, from knowing that I have an edge because I know I'm prepared.'

Rodriguez also knows the importance of staying in the present to find peak performance and the zone. Many other athletes also share his belief.

'Winners live in the present tense. People who come up short are consumed with future or past. I want to be living in the now.'

As Rodriguez approaches the mature years of his career his thoughts have drifted in the same direction as those of many other top athletes. There are arguments for and against the value of legacies. The importance of a belief system encompassing higher spiritual values is beyond question. However when the legacy becomes the overarching goal there is a real danger of moving away from staying in the present. Rodriquez clearly understands the importance of Now, so the legacy aspect requires careful balancing.

'There is a difference between image and reputation. Image is nice. Reputation is developed over an entire career. Reputation is what I'm searching for.'

Time will tell if Rodriguez can create the reputation that he would choose as his legacy. Time will also tell if the creation of this legacy enhances or detracts from his form and his peak performance.

Sports fans are demanding of their stars, and their expectations may be shallower than they and the athletes they fete would like to believe. When the career of the athlete is over, their playing record and statistics usually carry more weight with fans than their reputation. It is a very special athlete who earns both. Then they truly are a legend.

The Big Secret

Rodriguez's personal and sporting life have been anything but stable. Yet through all this volatility there has been one enduring constant, and that is that Rodriguez has maintained his astonishing form. He has stated many times the importance of Now, of living in the present tense.

Sports psychologists refer to this as 'staying in the present', and this is my suggestion as Rodriguez's special secret. It is something that he can do better than almost anybody else. If you are thinking of the mistake you made five minutes ago these thoughts will take you away from the zone. Even thoughts about the brilliant goal you just scored are equally damaging. Similarly thoughts about the future of what you will do with the prize money, or the party you will organise to celebrate your wonderful victory are likely to ensure that you seize defeat from the jaws of victory.

So what are the secrets of staying in the present, and how can you use them to increase your performance?

Almost all the work I do with clients can be summed up by the words 'staying in the present.' Finding as many ways as possible to switch off the conscious mind and all its worries and negativity.

Staying in the present is critical to performing well in sport, and in any other area of life. Generally people spend too long worrying about events from the past that continue to drag them back. They similarly spend hours worrying about events in the future that may or may not happen.

The same is true in sport. If you allow your mind to flutter like a butterfly backwards and forwards it does not allow any room for concentration in the present. Worse still the past memories we dredge up are usually negative, of the mistakes we have made. These memories develop a life of their own and catapult forward to thoughts of future outcomes. The usual result is a self-fulfilling prophecy of failure in the present.

So, what can you do to avoid these dangers? A good starting point is to adopt the mantra of 'focus on process and let the results take care of themselves.' Consider your sport, and list ten daily processes that would define a successful day. Processes are different to results.

A result might be to finish in the top ten, reduce your lap time by two seconds, or increase your success statistics for taking penalties. However in reality these results are largely outside your control. There are many reasons why it may not be possible on the day to hit your targets. So there is no point you worrying about it.

However, you are in control of your processes, and one process may be to arrive ten minutes early each day for training, and spend more time than the others on your warm-up routine. Apart from the fitness benefits you will also feel good because of the extra effort you have made.

Follow the same steps with your nine other key processes. Evaluate these processes at the end of the day. Have you followed them all perfectly? If so, you have done all you can do. Give yourself a reward.

After a week of similar success give yourself a bigger reward. If you are lucky your coach will reward you too. After a year it is certain that you will have more positive results, just by following and reinforcing your daily processes.

An enlightened coach will set and reward process goals, not issue mindless orders such as to score twenty goals each season. Remove the stress and the athletes often exceed their coach's and their own expectations. Success comes from doing the little things right, every time, by staying in the present. Another word for this approach is mindfulness. Mindfulness can be taught, and improves with regular practice. Developing processes for your sport will be a great start. So will be bringing in some help.

Almost all top athletes have mind coaches, and recognise the critical role they have played in their success. It surprises me that it is still often necessary to remind athletes that mind coaching is not for those who lack mental strength; it is for those who have already proven their resilience in sport, or in any other area of their life.

Successful people are not afraid to discover just how much higher they can climb.

Those who ignore the importance of mind coaching will never reach their potential, which is a great shame. We can all think of examples of players who were more than good enough to win a Major or equivalent title, but never did.

As previously noted another process you can adopt is to learn breathing techniques. As a Certified HeartMath® Sports Professional I am increasingly convinced of the vital role that breathing techniques play, and how they can help to stay in the present. I use them myself every day, and with all my clients. This is an extract from Science of the Heart,

'For centuries, the heart has been considered the source of emotion, courage and wisdom. At the Institute of HeartMath (IHM) Research Center, we are exploring the physiological mechanisms by which the heart communicates with the brain, thereby influencing information processing, perceptions, emotions and health. We are asking questions such as: Why do people experience the feeling or sensation of love and other positive emotional states in the area of the heart and what are the physiological ramifications of these emotions? How do stress and different emotional states affect the autonomic nervous system, the hormonal and immune systems, the heart and brain?.......

.... The answers to many of our original questions now provide a scientific basis to explain how and why the heart affects mental clarity, creativity, emotional balance and personal effectiveness. Our research and that of others indicate that the heart is far more than a simple pump. The heart is, in fact, a highly complex, self-organised information processing centre with its own functional "brain" that communicates with and influences the cranial brain via the nervous system, hormonal system and other pathways.

These influences profoundly affect brain function and most of the body's major organs, and ultimately determine the quality of life.'

HeartMath have a wonderful website, and much of their information is free. It is well worth a visit. Just because some of the techniques are simple does not mean they are not extremely effective.

Another reason why we find it so hard sometimes to stay in the present is because we think too much, and usually about the wrong things. When our brains are busy it is difficult if not impossible to stay in the present. Our brains are very like computers. We can only handle so much information at any one time. When our brains are overloaded they slow down, or even freeze, just like the dreaded PC 'blue screen of death.'

So what does this have to do with finding the zone? A great deal. Staying in the zone is a state of mind, and therefore dependent on how many things we are thinking about at any one time, and the state of health of our mind. A conscientious computer owner runs only those programmes that are being worked on, and defragments his or her hard disc regularly, freeing up space and increasing processing power. So how can you clean up your brain, and only think of the important things that will improve your performance?

The more information you move from the conscious to the unconscious areas of your brain the higher will be your performance level. This is true for any area of your life, at home, in sport, or at work. This is the role of practice, allowing skills to become automatic, and definitely not forcing them to be.

Thus if our success depends on the quality of our thoughts, and our thoughts depend on the power of our brain, then there are some very obvious steps we can take to increase our chances of success. The simplest step is to limit the amount of information we allow in.

The choices are simple, and there are only three. We either act on information, file it away, or delete it. Another word for this is concentration, which can behave like a cat. Concentration is a vital tool in any sport.

Contrary to what we might say to others, we do not lose our concentration. Unfortunately at any one time there are just too many places for it to go to. It is not lost, it has just gone somewhere else.

The truth is that people are most happy when they are totally absorbed in just one task. Time flies, the ego is for once subservient, and we become almost totally unaware of our environment. Without consciously recognising it we have unconsciously entered a magical self-hypnotic state.

However, unfortunately our normal state of mind is chaotic, which does not feel so comfortable. This chaos should not come as a surprise. We have never been so surrounded by so much up-to-the-second information. This information bombards us from TV, radio, newspapers, social network contacts, breaking news, text messages, telephones, diary reminders, and emails. So if you want to find the optimum state of mind how can you limit the information you allow in?

One answer is to switch these distractions off, at least while you are doing something else. There is nothing more certain to break concentration, or a zone experience, than a single interruption. A Zen expression is that there is nothing more certain to interfere with the straight flight of an arrow than a single thought.

The reason that you lost your concentration, or more accurately that it went somewhere else, is that the interruption will have exceeded your seven packets of information. Scientists have established that we can only process seven thoughts at once. The result is likely to be poor decisions, a sense of energy draining away, and the pleasure of the moment lost forever. Quite simply, multitasking does not work. Leonardo da Vinci considered simplicity as the ultimate sophistication, despite being the leading scholar of his time in almost every known discipline.

Many people believe they can multitask effectively, and become rather vociferous when challenged on this subject. There are occasions when they are totally correct. If the tasks are simple and repetitive they can be safely left to the unconscious, and will likely be performed the better for it.

However, when it is necessary to make important decisions based upon complex information, concentration is required. The cat needs to be herded. This concentration involves the effective mobilisation of an exquisite balance of both conscious and unconscious thought.

You will almost certainly be painfully surprised by how hard you find it to switch off all your information gathering toys. When was the last time you switched them off for more than twelve hours? Many people struggle with 12 minutes.

This chapter has explored the chaotic mess that we call our brain. If it were a wheelie bin there is no way we could close the lid on it because of its overflowing contents. Much of this rubbish is worthless, even though we may not know it. Sadly the precious gold nuggets that hide within this morass may be lost from sight for ever. These nuggets are priceless, because they will lead you to the zone. What better time than now for a thorough spring clean?

'It is only when we silent the blaring sounds of our daily existence that we can finally hear the whispers of truth that life reveals to us, as it stands knocking on the doorsteps of our hearts.' K.T. Jong

Formula One racing driver Fernando Alonso has also found his moments of silence in his otherwise noisy world, as we will discover in the next chapter.

Scratch Box

Chapter 8 - Fernando Alonso

Highlights

Fernando Alonso Díaz is a Spanish Formula One racing driver. He has won the coveted World Championship on two consecutive occasions. He was the youngest driver to achieve this honour, and so he is rightfully considered one of the greatest drivers ever.

Alonso is also the owner of an unusual tattoo on his back. It is an ancient samurai warrior, representing strength, intelligence, and the will to win. These qualities were described by Yamamoto Tsunetomo, in his spiritual guide for a warrior titled Hagakure, also known as The Book of the Samurai. It was written in the eighteenth century.

The book describes the warrior code, known as Bushido. Its essence is the philosophy that a warrior should consider himself already dead. Those that achieve this state of mind describe it as a freedom from earthly worries, with the result that all their mental and physical energy can be directed at the task in hand.

Most coaches would not encourage their clients to develop their thoughts to this morbid extreme. However, most would agree that peak performance comes from the mental discipline of staying in the present. The events of the past and the future are of no concern, so encouraging a pure focus of concentration and enlightenment.

This viewpoint echoes one of the Zen foundations concerning the danger of over-attachment to people and possessions, leading inevitably to fear of their loss. The result of such earthly fears act as barriers to peak performance. In the sporting world athletes often describe their triumphs as arising from discovering the joy of letting go, having no fear of failure, keeping things simple, and abandoning ego.

Fame and fortune are not the easiest gifts to accept and control, especially at an early age. There is nothing more certain to deflect focus than to succumb to the stupefying siren voices of flattery. However Alonso has kept his feet firmly grounded.

‘Formula One is a strange world but if you have clear values, you can maintain the separation between truth and fiction. If people praise you, you cannot let it go to your head, because at the next race you could be criticised.’

Values are the solid foundation of personality and performance. Not all athletes have developed or inherited values, and some have been very successful without them. However most of the best of the best recognise that values have been the guiding light throughout their career, and have also extended its length.

When an athlete’s fortune has been secured, it is his or her values that provide the spur to continue to train, to compete, and to break records. Enduring values provide a sense of purpose and a reason to get out of bed each day.

It is unclear how much research Alonso has pursued into Eastern philosophies. However it is certain that he is well aware of the risks of his chosen sport. The 1970s’ were called the killing years in motor sport, and with good reason. A driver had only a one in three chance of surviving, and so Alonso will know only too well the dangers of his sport, about the deaths of friends and fellow competitors, not to mention spectators too.

Thankfully driver safety has improved dramatically since those black years, not least because of the efforts of drivers such as Sir Jackie Stewart, and individuals such as Professor Sid Watkins who took control of safety at Formula One circuits following the death of his close friend Ayrton Senna. There were no subsequent deaths in Formula One from this point on. Even so Formula One is still a dangerous sport, and Alonso will be aware of the calculated risks that he faces every time he is strapped into his car. As Samuel Johnson wrote, the fear of imminent death ‘concentrates his mind wonderfully.’

Apart from racing cars Alonso's other passion is for performing card tricks. The connection between Formula One and performing card tricks is not an obvious one. Perhaps the concentration required for card tricks is the perfect antidote to combat the stresses of life in the fast lane.

Another secret to Alonso's success is a rare gift, and one which many athletes share. It is to keep life simple. He describes his career as,

'For me it's a simple sport and a simple way to live these seven or eight years of maximum sport.'

This simplicity extends to his own performance in the cockpit of his car, and forms a buffer to reduce the inevitable stresses that fame, fortune, and the risk of sudden death bring.

'For me, tomorrow will be another day whether I finish first or last. I have to do the maximum and I cannot ask any more from myself.'

Most people worry too much about their results, leading to loss of confidence, and more poor results. Focus on process, do the best you can, and then you do not need to explain your actions to yourself, or to anyone else either.

The Big Secret

Zen is a word used many times in connection with sport and rightfully so. Just as with meditation, it has many different definitions. Zen is a branch of Buddhism, in which meditation forms a central tenet. It is not a religion, but a philosophy. In its purest sense deep insights are transmitted from coach to client not by speech, or words, but by thought. It is like an intuition, instinct, or gut feeling.

Whether this is true or not we all know people that we are comfortable being with, and who make us feel relaxed and confident. We may refer to such people as 'being on the same wavelength.'

D T Suzuki is widely credited as the author who was able to explain Zen in a pragmatic way that would be more easily understandable to Western cultures. In his Essays in Zen Buddhism he wrote,

'All that one can do in the way of communicating the experience to others is to suggest or indicate, and this is only tentatively. The one who has had it understands when such indications are given, but when we try to have a glimpse of it through the indices given we utterly fail.'

Zen philosophy is complex, and it is beyond the scope of this book to express anything more than a few simple ideas. Even so, if you are able to selectively follow one or more key Zen principles it is very likely that you will be calmer, gain greater control of your emotions, find the zone, and perform closer to the limits of your potential.

For example, as previously mentioned, Zen teaches that a universal human failing is our over-attachment to objects and outcomes. Conversely, detachment results in less pressure and greater calm. Missing a penalty should not spoil your football match, neither will scoring it make much difference either. Life by its nature is ebb and flow. Enjoy the good times while they last, and keep your spirits up during the difficult times. They cannot last for ever.

Suzuki is very clear that to excel in sport it is not enough to have ability and to practice. He wrote,

'In Japan, perhaps as in other countries too, mere technical knowledge of an art is not enough to make man its master; he ought to have delved into the inner spirit of it. This spirit is grasped only when his mind is in complete harmony with the principle of life itself, that is, when he attains to a certain state of mind known as mushin, 'no mind.' In Buddhist phraseology, it means going beyond the dualism of all forms of life and death, good and evil, being and non-being.'

D.T. Suzuki's foreword to Eugen Herrigel's Zen in the Art of Archery describes the dangers of thinking too much, and becoming over-technical. Perfectionism and sport do not always coexist in comfort. If he is right then we need to go back and play sport as a child would. He probably is right, as many athletes who lose their form express a wish that they could go back, and play as they did when they were young.

'As soon as we reflect, deliberate, and conceptualise, the original unconsciousness is lost and a thought interferes... The arrow is off the string but does not fly straight on the target, nor does the target stand where it is. Calculation, which is miscalculation, set in... Man is a thinking reed but his great works are done when he is not calculating and thinking. 'Childlikeness' has to be restored with long years of training in self-forgetfulness.'

If you wish to read more about this fascinating subject I recommend an excellent review article, Zen Buddhism, Sport Psychology and Golf, by Simon Jenkins [6].

There are many similarities between the chapters on meditation, staying in the present, and Zen. Adopt any one point and it is very likely that your performance will move to the next level, adopt two or more and it is certain.

Often all that is necessary is to be more in touch with our world, moment by moment, and this will be a constant strand throughout this book. Author Robert Pirsig and his book Zen & the Art of Motorcycle Maintenance has provided me with much inspiration since my student days. Although his messages are not the easiest to decipher, I think I know (but easily could be wrong) what he means about our search for truth.

'It is a puzzling thing. The truth knocks on the door and you say, "Go away, I'm looking for the truth," and so it goes away. Puzzling.'

Scratch Box

Chapter 9 - Mahendra Singh Dhoni

Highlights

Mahendra Singh Dhoni is the current captain of the Indian cricket team. He is the highest paid cricketer in the world, earning an estimated $26 million during 2012. He made his international debut in 2004, and was appointed captain of India in 2007 at the age of 26. This is an unusually young age for one of the most challenging roles in world cricket.

Dhoni's extraordinary progress has continued, and under his inspirational leadership India won the 2007 ICC World Twenty20 in 2007-08, and the 2011 World Cup. India also climbed to No. 1 in the ICC Test Rankings in December 2009. He is the most successful Indian captain in history in the One Day and Test formats of international cricket.

Not only does Dhoni command the total respect of his cricket-loving Indian nation, but also has been awarded the highest praise from his players, not least the legendary Sachin Tendulkar and Sourav Ganguly.

Tendulkar considered Dhoni to be the best captain he has played under. He felt that he created an aura of calm that transmitted to his players, even under the most extreme pressure. Tendulkar went further and praised Dhoni as India's best ever captain.

Dhoni is an inspirational leader, and produces peak performance not only in his own game, but also with his players. How does he do this? What makes him stand head and shoulders above his peers at the highest level of cricket? Extracts from his numerous interviews offer some intriguing clues. These are some of his comments that relate to the importance of the team, rather than the individual.

- The leader should be humble, and part of the team
- All team members deserve respect and trust
- The team is more important than any individual
- Any member of the team, even if in poor form, is capable of a match-winning performance at any time.
- Share all credit with the team, and praise them in public
- Performance speaks louder than words

Great teams are not made by copying what others do. Doing something different takes courage, and is a hallmark of successful individuals. Einstein defined insanity as repeating the same mistakes, each time hoping for a different result, and yet that is so often what people do. It is because they prefer to stick to the familiar, and lack the courage or the imagination to experiment. Dhoni is an exception. He places great weight on the importance of creating a supportive environment that encourages experimentation, and taking calculated risks.

Dhoni also wisely avoids the temptation to predict the future, which he knows is beyond his control. He saves his energy for what he and his team can control, namely their emotions and their processes.

'I never predict what will happen in cricket. We believe in each other and we believe in the process. We will take each game in the right frame of mind,' he said.

'We are not thinking about what may happen if we achieve or what may happen if we don't succeed because those two things are beyond our control. So rather than thinking about something that's too much ahead of us it is very important to take every game in the right frame of mind and that is what will be our process throughout the tournament.'

Dhoni is a perfect example of the power of the empty mind. It is not full of thoughts about technique, results, or statistics. His mind holds on to only a few things that are far more important, such as having fun, staying in the present, focussing on process, and letting the results take care of themselves. Dhoni has been described as a yogi on the cricket field.

The Big Secret

Arguably Dhoni's greatest ability is to live in the present, and to pass this gift to his team. It is a central tenet of many sports, and sometimes referred to as mindfulness. It is a gift that comes most easily to members of Eastern cultures, but can be cultivated in all, though not without some effort. Living in the present allows focus, encourages peak performance, and so is worthy of further study.

There are many different ways to stay in the present, and one that certainly applies to Dhoni is to have a sense of fun and create happiness. This is Dhoni's secret, being happy. Too often athletes believe that they should always be serious, and do not realise that this acts as a barrier to the child within, preventing their peak performance.

Happiness and peak performance are linked. Happy athletes usually reach their sporting potential much easier than unhappy ones. Athletes also feel happy as a result of performing well, so reinforcing the cycle of peak performance.

We all have more opportunities for finding happiness through sports and leisure than in any other area of our life. There are several very good reasons why this should be so. Sport has been around for as long as humans. When two people gather one will always boast that he can throw a rock further, fire an arrow straighter, jump higher, and run faster than his friend.

This natural sense of competition is in our genes too. Natural selection favours competitive individuals because they are more likely to succeed in life and pass on these genes to future generations. Such people raise the bar of expectations and progress.

Competition leads to accidents too, sometimes with serious consequences. However, overall the impersonal laws of natural selection consider this a price worth paying for the advancement of the human race.

Fortunately most of the time competition is fun. However simple the activity, happiness results. Curiously the rules of such simple skirmishes are a lot more complicated than they appear. They may not be even written down, but passed down from one generation to the next.

So over the years the rules evolve so that both parties have a chance of success. This provides challenge, opportunities to try new techniques, and a clear goal, to win and claim the prize or the bragging rights.

The competitors focus on the task, lose sense of time, forget about the worries of their life for a few minutes, and are happy. The reason they are happy is that experts through the ages have deliberately designed such activities with this point in mind.

Sport has been and always will be woven into the fabric of our lives.There is something about sport that resonates at a deeper level of the human psyche. Sport provides an opportunity to transcend everyday existence, and provide the ultimate opportunity for mind, body, and soul to combine as one.

The moment is your only infinitesimally small contact with the real world, and this is where happy people live. The rest of time is either history, or the future. Neither of which you control.

Dhoni understands this more than most people, and his happiness keeps him firmly rooted in the moment, and infects the rest of his team too. This is why he is such an inspirational leader. Usain Bolt is the subject of our next chapter. He is also a very happy man, and the fastest too.

Scratch Box

Chapter 10 - Usain Bolt

Highlights

Usain Bolt was born in Jamaica, and is the most well known athlete in the world. He currently holds the world record at both 100 metres and 200 metres, as well as in the 4 x 100 metres relay.

Despite his relaxed and easy going personality he is also a genuine entertainer. Not only does he have a huge fan base within athletics, but he has also attracted millions of new fans who would not normally be interested in this sport. For all these reasons he earns more than any other athlete in history.

Bolt approached the London 2012 Olympics under something of a cloud. His recent form had been indifferent by his standards, and there were persistent rumours of injury and training setbacks. Equally worryingly he had been disqualified controversially in the heats of the 2011 World Championships, for a false start. Who knew what this might have done to his confidence?

Even at the best of times Bolt knew that he was not a good starter. This had always been a source of considerable worry to him, until his coach reassured him that all would be well. He repeated again that Bolt's success was his phenomenal acceleration in the latter stages of the race. Even if his rivals were ahead at the start they would not be able to match his blistering pace at the end of the race. Perhaps this approach would be helpful for you too. Unlike most people, focus on what you are really good at, and not your imperfections.

So it proved in London 2012, when Bolt set a new world record of 9.63 seconds. The crowd were delighted with his antics. His huge smile, his relaxed chatter to the volunteer at the blocks, his play acting for the TV cameras, the Bolt victory pose, and his five push ups at the end of the race to celebrate his five gold medals. In his post-race interview he reiterated,

'I won because I stopped worrying about my start.'

Again, as in 2008, Bolt was able to slow down in the last few strides. This time he held his left finger to his mouth, a signal for his critics to be quiet. They had made the mistake of writing off his chances again, as they had in 2008. Then Bolt had told them that they should also have listened, because he kept repeating in his many interviews before the race that he would win.

So what are the secrets of Bolt's stellar performance? In some ways they are difficult to unearth because he says there are no secrets, but perhaps this is also his greatest secret. He keeps things simple, and does not paralyse his mind with technical thoughts. He does not have a special diet, and eats and drinks whatever he fancies. In the starting blocks he claims to think about what kind of pizza he will order later that evening

In a recent TV interview Bolt was asked for his five top tips for sprinters. He listed them:

1. Be fast out of the blocks.
2. Move easily through transition.
3. Run tall at the end of the race.

His interviewer politely pointed out that this was only three tips. Usain looked puzzled, and finally replied that he could not think of any more, that running fast was just as simple as that, and there was no need to complicate it further. In other interviews he sparingly releases other clues. He stays relaxed before a race, and only focuses when he is in the blocks, and describes this state as 'tunnel vision.'

Bolt sometimes lacks motivation for the harsh training that is required, and counters this by repeated affirmations to himself, such as 'I am the Best.' Affirmations work at the unconscious level, with the result that his mind accepts that to be the best requires commitment to train harder than his closest rivals.

There are other secrets to Bolt's success, secrets that he does not think are anything special, because they are so obvious to him, and he remains innocently unaware that they are not so obvious to most other people. The following examples highlight the mind set of a champion, and time spent considering how you could apply them to your sport, work, or personal life will be repaid many times over.

Pick the right coach, who will explain what you need to know, not what you want to hear. A coach who understands that peak performance demands the exquisite balance of physical, technical, mental and spiritual qualities. Bolt knew that his relaxed approach to life could be his greatest danger, or greatest strength. He chose Mills because he knew that his tough disciplined approach would bring out his best qualities, and harden him to compete against the best at the highest level.

Bolt has suffered many injuries during his career, and all athletes fear injury. Mills stressed to Bolt that whilst injuries were not to be welcomed, nor were they to be feared. The injuries demonstrated that Bolt was pushing the limits of his body, and discovering just how good he could be.

Bolt has not always enjoyed success, and has been beaten many times, especially at the start of his career. Many athletes never learn how to handle defeat. It triggers defensive behaviours, and stifles enjoyment. Successful athletes have all handled defeat and turned it to their advantage, as an opportunity to learn. They can then compete without fear, knowing that all possible consequences have positive benefits. It is therefore not a surprise that the no fear mindset increases the chances of winning, when winning is a consequence of doing other things right, rather than a goal in itself. Bolt describes it as,

'You have to learn how to lose before you can learn how to win.'

The aim for all athletes it to treat all races the same, whether in practice or the Olympic finals. Keep to the same routines, rather than special preparations for the most important events. As mentioned previously, Bolt is an entertainer. This suits his personality, with the added benefit that it is also a great way to reduce stress. It is always preferable to think of something pleasant, rather than how important the race will be to your future.

Another secret you can adopt is to train with a friend who is at least as committed to winning as you are, and performs almost as well. This is a powerful tool to add spice to practice, and prevents complacency. Yohan Blake performs this role perfectly for Bolt, and presumably Blake believes it helps his preparation too. Long distance runner Mo Farah has a similar relationship with Galen Rupp.

Never underestimate the power of laughter. Always keep in mind that life is meant to be fun. If your job or sport is the equivalent of day jail then change it. Willpower alone will not produce results. Bolt already has more money than he will ever need, and so runs for fun. Setting new world records is almost incidental, and just a welcome byproduct of doing what he likes doing, and which he does better than any other human being.

The Big Secret

Bolt has mastered many secrets of success. The one secret that stands out the most is that above all he keeps things simple. This is a mark of true genius. Renowned economist E.F. Schumacher would surely agree too.

'Any intelligent fool can make things bigger, more complex, and more violent. It takes a touch of genius - and a lot of courage - to move in the opposite direction.'

There was a time when life was much more simple for you, though it was a long time ago, when you were a baby. From the very first day you were 99.99% ready for life. You needed parental support, but all your systems and organs were formed, and functioning perfectly.

You did not need to think about your insulin metabolism, or your immune system, because they were automatic. They were governed by your unconscious mind.

You did not really have a conscious mind at this point, but you soon began to acquire one.

Although it was only small, your conscious mind soon felt that it was the most important thing in your life, and was the boss. It is not a coincidence, but this is when your life also became more complicated.

You enjoyed playing games from the time you could walk, and did not worry about how to run, or how to hold a stick with the correct grip.

As children your decisions were simple and made by reflex. Surprisingly often they were also correct decisions. As we grow older we do not necessarily grow wiser, even though it may appear so. However as we grow older we are more aware of the wide range of choices that are available, and life is not so simple any more.

The danger is that with choice comes the opportunity and temptation to construct an egocentric world. Even ordering a coffee now presents multiple choices. Make the right choice and you feel great. Make the wrong one, or even a good but not a perfect choice, and you are left feeling disappointed and unfulfilled.

This was just a simple example about simplicity. What is more important is that preoccupation with self, and what others may think of you, drains energy, and is more likely to destroy self-esteem than to enhance confidence. It is another barrier to peak sports performance too.

It is very likely that Bolt would agree with Terri Guillemets when she stated that,

'Life is amazingly good when it's simple and amazingly simple when it's good.'

Scratch Box

Chapter 11 - Confidence

I have saved the most important ingredient of peak performance for last. It is confidence. This is not to imply in any way that the ten ingredients in the preceding chapters are not important. They certainly are, but in isolation they are worthless.

With confidence, anything is possible. Without confidence, little is possible. It is as simple as that. Confidence is the catalyst that ignites the ten other ingredients to produce an explosion of sporting creativity.

The ten sporting stars highlighted in the previous chapters all possess massive confidence, perhaps even to the point of arrogance. That is why they are all successful, rich, and hopefully happy too.

Confidence will be vital for you too. You may not feel very confident right now, and compare yourself critically with others. Join the club, everybody, or almost everybody, feels the same. However, most people do not talk about it. It is a taboo subject. A badge of shame, and an admission of failure. What utter nonsense.

We are all the same because we are genetically programmed to be so. So where is the shame in that? Homo sapiens owes its current success as the dominant species on this planet to its evolution, or creation, as a social animal.

If we all had bucketfuls of confidence can you imagine what kind of world we might live in? Even living in the same house with such a creature can be a nightmare. Fortunately all that is required is just a little more confidence.

Putting it another way, our brains have been scrambled somewhere in our history. Thousands of years ago we worried about important things like weather, wild animals, and the hostile tribe on the other side of the hill. Now, at least in the developed world, we worry that our neighbour has a bigger car than we do, that we have developed another wrinkle on our face, or laid down another few grammes of fat around our waist.

If I ever had any doubt about the importance of confidence it was massively reinforced by the blockbuster success of my first audiobook. Its title was unusual, to say the least, Zen Hypnosis: Confidence. Indeed the publishers were worried that the title would scare potential buyers away.

Zen Hypnosis: Confidence was released on iTunes in late 2009. It charted almost immediately, and reached number one in the self development section in UK in January 2010, where it stayed for most of the year. Indeed for long periods it was the top seller in any genre, even outselling Dan Brown's latest title. It has remained in the charts ever since.

So what did this tell me? First, that despite this audiobook being far from the best product out there, it sold more copies than any of the other more prestigious titles. The reason, I believe, was that the word 'confidence' in the title resonated with many people. The relative anonymity of buying internet downloads compared to buying in a bookshop was probably another factor too. It has transformed beyond recognition the lives of some listeners. It provided the catalyst for change that some people were searching for. It gave them a nudge. It empowered them at a deep level, so that they could do the rest for themselves.

So I hope I have convinced you of the importance of confidence, and the reasons why most people feel that they do not have enough confidence. Now I can share with you some very practical steps that you can take to increase your confidence levels. Then the rest is up to you, and I wish you every success.

What you see in the mirror every morning will dictate what you feel about yourself, whether it be good or bad. It may be your physical appearance, or your assessment of your personality, or what you have achieved in your life. Sadly, for many people, their assessment of themselves will be highly critical.

'Our doubts are traitors, and make us lose the good we oft might win, by fearing to attempt.' William Shakespeare, Measure for Measure, 1604

Unfortunately such harsh self-criticism destroys confidence, which further reinforces this cycle of negativity. This will not help your search for success. It will not help you find the intuitive mindset that will unleash peak performance. So how can you break this destructive cycle? Fortunately it may be easier than you think.

Internal Dialogue

A great place to start is your internal dialogue, sometimes called self-talk. This is the voice that you have in your brain. There is often a constant chatter giving a running commentary of your life. Very often it slips out of the mouth, usually followed by an embarrassed pause. 'I was just talking to myself,' you mutter.

Confidence is a state of mind, and therefore to a greater or lesser extent under your control. Your thoughts control your mood, and very often what goes on in your head comes out in your life. As previously mentioned, Henry Ford expressed this succinctly,

'Whether you think you can or think you can't - you are right.'

If you think something bad will happen to you the chances are that you will not be surprised when it does. Fortunately the opposite is also true. Develop a positive attitude, value your talents, approach challenges in this light, and your chances of success have increased significantly, further strengthening your confidence for future challenges. This is how you can help yourself. Adopt this simple mantra right now. Say it out aloud.

'From this moment forward I will only say good things about myself.'

If you are concerned that you might lose out on learning from your mistakes, or becoming arrogant you can add the following words if you so wish.

'Fear not. I can trust family, friends, and the rest of the world to point out my mistakes. I do not need to give them any help.'

Remember The Good Times

There are other ways to increase your confidence and self-esteem too. As with most things in life it will require some preparation, and effort on your part. However when compared to the size of the glittering prize out there it will be one of the best investments you have ever made.

A powerful starting point is to make this commitment. Write it down, and then you are much more likely to keep to it. Say it out aloud too, with conviction.

'From this moment forward I will remember every good thing that happens to me.'

Unfortunately most people have a brilliant memory for remembering all the things that went wrong, but struggle to think of the many good things that have gone right in their lives.

So when somebody says something complimentary to you, wallow in the pleasure for a second or two longer than you ordinarily would, before allowing the memory to slip into your unconscious mind. If you can do this several times a day for a month there will be a subtle change in your brain chemistry and outlook on life. You will notice the difference. Those closest to you will notice it more.

You can enhance the effect by subtly giving your brain another push in the right direction. When you have one of these pleasurable experiences make sure that the memory is easy to retrieve by associating it with a physical anchor.

Some people touch their thumb and forefinger together to reinforce a happy memory. Others touch their ear, or brush their trousers. Spend some time choosing yours. It should be discreet, but most importantly it should feel right with you. Adopt this practice for a month, and the chances are that you will continue in the future. These anchors will become a seamless and automatic part of your life.

Look Like You Feel – Feel Like You Look

There are many other powerful tools to enrich confidence. Think for a moment of a person who is nervous, or how you might look and feel when worried about something.

A nervous person trembles, adopts a withdrawn posture, with head held down. Eyes move quickly, as do all other body parts. This arousal is due to the physiological changes associated with overstimulation of the autonomic sympathetic nervous system, and the resultant effects of adrenalin and other hormones.

This is known as the 'Fight or Flight' Response. If we hooked this person up to a biological monitor we would record many other physiological changes, including an increased heart rate, increased breathing rate, increased blood pressure, sweaty palms, and dry mouth.

These changes prepare the body for instant action, and in the short-term are thus valuable. However in our modern society much of our stress is due to emotional factors, rather than physical causes that require immediate physical effort. The result is that we do not burn off the adrenalin and other hormones, and so live in a constant state of stress and arousal. The medical consequences may be dire, and include higher risks of hypertension, heart problems, anxiety, depression, and even cancer.

The personal consequences are equally as dire. You will find it difficult, if not impossible, to connect to your unconscious mind. You will not find the open door to the zone, and may even be drawn to the doors that are best left alone.

Stress is a killer. It takes life, it spoils life, it gets in the way of everything that you can enjoy in life. The good news is that there are several ways to eliminate stress, or at least to control it.

The autonomic nervous system was thought to be beyond our conscious control. Now there is clear evidence that a degree of control is possible. This provides opportunities to overcome some of the dangerous effects of stress. For example Olympic pistol and rifle athletes, and archers have learnt how to control their heart rate to maintain a steady aim. Snooker and darts players have too, as have many top golfers.

One simple technique you can execute right now is to adopt a confident posture – the opposite of the previous nervous posture. Stand or sit tall, breathe deeply and slowly, move calmly, and smile. The mind can affect our physiology, and the opposite is equally true. Mind and body are seamlessly linked, and we can learn to use this to our advantage.

'Happiness is when what you think, what you say, and what you do are in harmony.' Dale Carnegie, (1888-1955), American writer.

Milton Erickson, the father of American medical hypnosis, also fully appreciated the effect of posture on confidence. He would instruct his chronically depressed patients to walk home, and count the chimneys on the way.

One reason for his curious directive is that doing something, especially if depressed, is always better than doing nothing. There is also no way to avoid looking up and adopting a tall posture when counting chimneys. Not surprisingly his patients reported feeling somewhat better, but they were not sure why!

Mental strategies to overcome and eventually master these natural physiological responses have been explored in more detail throughout this book. Such strategies include the role of breathing, meditation, posture, self-talk, confidence anchors, visualisation, and other ways to 'stay in the present.' All of these strategies, in one way or another, enhance confidence.

What You Think Is What You Get

Many, if not all, of the athletes studied in this book appreciate the importance of happiness to their confidence, and to their performance. It is seen in ordinary daily life too. Two people can share the same job, the same experiences, and yet at the end of the day feel completely different about it.

For example, Anne and Barbara work in the same office, performing similar jobs. When they finish work they decide to stop for a drink on the way home. Anne relates what a terrible day she has had, while Barbara says that she quite enjoyed her day.

So here we have two different people who shared the same experiences, but arrived at very different conclusions. We all know people like Anne and Barbara. Some people are naturally optimistic, others pessimistic. So our level of happiness is dependent to some degree on how we filter our everyday experiences. This affects what is loosely called our quality of life.

Anne has slammed shut the doors that surrounded her, while Barbara has left open many intriguing possibilities. Any one of them could change her life in unimagined ways.

Mahatma Ghandi was far more to the point.

'A person will be just about as happy as they make up their minds to be.'

As we grow older we do not necessarily grow wiser, even though it may appear so. As children our decisions are simple and made by reflex. Surprisingly often they are also correct decisions. However as we grow older we are more aware of the wide range of choices that are available, and life is not so simple any more.

Preoccupation with self, and what others may think of you, drains energy, and is more likely to destroy self-esteem than to enhance confidence.

A central tenet of many Eastern cultures is that letting go of ego counter-intuitively encourages personal growth and self-esteem. Western cultures sometimes refer to naturally confident people as being 'comfortable in their own skin.'

The top sports stars have all found different methods to let go of their ego, and as a result live more fully in the present, and surround themselves with an invincible aura of confidence. Adopt one or more of the confidence strategies described in this chapter and you will find the zone a lot more often, and stay there at least a little bit longer. Your performance levels will increase, and you will have a lot more fun too.

This table summarises the ten strategies to build confidence that the top athletes have exploited to their maximum potential. It is not exhaustive, but more than enough for a short book, and more than enough to raise your game to at least the next level too.

Name	The $447 Million Mind Secret
Mayweather	Power Goals
Woods	Meditation & The Zone
James	Control Of Emotions
Federer	Push Luck On Your Side
Ronaldo	Awesome Visualisation
Manning	Dealing With Adversity
Rodriguez	Staying In The Present
Alonso	Zen
Dhoni	Be Happy
Bolt	Keep It Simple

Scratch Box

Conclusion

What Next?

This book is deliberately not just a list of recommendations designed to propel your sports performance to at least the next level, although that should be a welcome benefit. It is the process that is important, and it is your processes that will produce results. It is not what has been written that will be the most important ingredient in your journey. Rather it will be your own thoughts that surface, as if from nowhere, that will guide you in what instinctively feels as if it is the right direction. These are the golden 'Mind Pops'.

My efforts have been limited to attempts to engage with your unconscious mind, plant a few ideas, and to put you in touch with the resources that will lead to your sporting development, and the successes that lie beyond.

What works for you may not work for another person, and vice versa. One thing is for sure.

- If you read the whole of this book it is possible you will find more success.
- If you also write down the key nuggets and your three action points at the end of each chapter it is probable you will find more success.
- If you also remind yourself daily about your action points from each chapter it is almost certain that you will find more success.
- If you also tell another person about your action points from each chapter it is guaranteed that you will find more success.

There is something else you may choose to do too, and it will be very powerful. Many successful business leaders have just one piece of paper on their desk, and they review it each morning. This paper is the distilled life essence of their empire – the few key critical factors that define success or failure. All are measurable, and the CEO is only happy when he has his or her finger on this pulse.

You too will benefit from a similar approach. Cut and paste all your chapter nuggets onto one piece of paper. Review this list every morning, and tick five items to action that day. Review it again at the end of each day, and record your score.

Even if you did not hit all of your targets, you will still feel happier than you might expect. It is because you have exercised a degree of control over your life, and that is something we all want more of.

Some clients have constructed mind maps or nodes that reinforce the visual impact of their action points. There are some great applications that you can download, and some of them are free too.

Remember the new born baby I mentioned in the Usain Bolt chapter? It was 99.99% complete, lacking only a conscious mind. Years later it has completed its development. Its conscious mind is now firmly in control, and has conveniently forgotten that it still only forms 0.01% of its existence.

This conscious mind was shaped as a result of life experiences, and in response to interactions with other people. Some of these experiences would have been positive, and others far less so. The degree of resultant success depends less on the pleasure associated with these experiences, but far more on how this person chooses to think about them.

How many open doors of opportunity were explored during its life, and how many remained unseen, or unopened, with the result that the riches beyond were lost for ever? Did this person move forward with its life and find success, or did it move backwards? Was the world a better place for its life, or for its passing?

Just to think of these things is likely to enrich your life, and your life is all that matters. It is the only life that you can control, even if only just a little. A little bit more control can make all the difference.

I sincerely hope that you have found at least one idea within this book that will lead you to greater success and more fun in your sport, whatever that might be. Perhaps you found many opportunities, or perhaps they eluded you. Either way, I would like to know. What would you do differently next time? What advice would you give to the next generation? Perhaps you will be a coach too? Who knows, you might even find that coaching others brings you more pleasure than your own sports career?

Please feel free to write to me with your comments through my website www.drstephensimpson.com. I reply personally to every note. If you have a question I will do my best to answer that too. Sign up for the regular newsletter, it is free and crammed with tips, insights from other readers, and sometimes free offers too. Even better, write a short article, and I'll do my best to publish it.

Whichever route you take I wish you a pleasant journey, and hope that the success and happiness you find at your sporting destination exceeds your wildest expectations.

Safe travels.

References

1. Mayweather: I'm better than Ali was. Reuters - Wed, 28 Apr 2010
2. http://www.sisport.com/sisport/files/Talent%20Document%20-%20Mindset%20(Web).pdf
3. http://www.youtube.com/watch?v=QEaWv0SBp3A&feature=player_embedded
4. http://en.wikipedia.org/wiki/LeBron_James
5. http://www.evancarmichael.com/Famous-Entrepreneurs/643/Howard-Schultz-Starbucks.html
6. Jenkins, S (2008). Annual Review of Golf Coaching. Zen Buddhism, Sport Psychology and Golf, 215-236. Brentwood, UK. Multi-Science Publishing

About The Author

Dr. Stephen Simpson is a medical specialist, MBA, and Fellow of the Royal Society of Medicine. He works as an elite performance coach, and has written and presented many scientific papers at international conferences, as well as making frequent guest appearances on TV and radio. His clients include leading names from the world of sport, business, and the entertainment industries.

Dr. Simpson is also a bestselling book and audiobook author and presenter. Full details can be found on his website www.drstephensimpson.com.

www.ingramcontent.com/pod-product-compliance
Ingram Content Group UK Ltd.
Pitfield, Milton Keynes, MK11 3LW, UK
UKHW020139250726
13967UKWH00002B/747